LOVE
GOES
F1RST

LOVE GOES F1RST

REACHING OTHERS IN AN AGE OF ANXIETY AND DIVISION

ANDREW FORREST

ZONDERVAN
REFLECTIVE

SEEDBED

ZONDERVAN REFLECTIVE

Love Goes First
Copyright © 2025 by David Andrew Forrest

Published by Zondervan, 3950 Sparks Drive SE, Suite 101, Grand Rapids, MI 49546, USA.
Zondervan is a registered trademark of The Zondervan Corporation, L.L.C., a wholly owned
subsidiary of HarperCollins Christian Publishing, Inc.

Requests for information should be addressed to customercare@harpercollins.com.

Zondervan titles may be purchased in bulk for educational, business, fundraising, or sales
promotional use. For information, please email SpecialMarkets@Zondervan.com.

ISBN 978-0-310-11943-2 (audio)

Library of Congress Cataloging-in-Publication Data
Names: Forrest, Andrew, 1980- author.
Title: Love goes first : reaching others in an age of anxiety and division / Andrew Forrest.
Description: Grand Rapids, Michigan : Zondervan Reflective, [2025]
Identifiers: LCCN 2025007077 (print) | LCCN 2025007078 (ebook) | ISBN 9780310119418 paperback
   | ISBN 9780310119425 ebook
Subjects: LCSH: Love—Religious aspects—Christianity. | Caring—Religious aspects—Christianity.
   | Neighborliness—Religious aspects—Christianity.
Classification: LCC BV4639 .F584 2025 (print) | LCC BV4639 (ebook) | DDC 248.4—dc23
   /eng/20250430
LC record available at https://lccn.loc.gov/2025007077
LC ebook record available at https://lccn.loc.gov/2025007078

HarperCollins Publishers, Macken House, 39/40 Mayor Street Upper,
Dublin 1, D01 C9W8, Ireland (https://www.harpercollins.com)

Cover design: Tammy Johnson
Interior design: Emily Ghattas

$PrintCode

Elaine, Jack, and Annie:
this is for you

Every one of us came into the world looking for one thing: the moment we were born we were looking for a face. We were born and in the shock and surprise of birth we opened our eyes and we looked for a face, because until we see a face—until another sees us—we do not know who we are, and we looked for someone who would look at us. . . . Every human being . . . is looking for someone who is looking for us.

—ANDY CROUCH, "OVERCOMING OUR GREATEST AFFLICTION"

CONTENTS

INTRODUCTION

"What Do We Do Now?"

There is this great scene at the end of the 1972 satirical political movie *The Candidate*, which is about a man (played by Robert Redford) who runs for the United States Senate in California believing that he has no chance of winning and therefore nothing to lose. Because he doesn't expect victory, he is surprised to find himself on election night having just been elected senator from California. Robert Redford's character is dumbfounded and overwhelmed by the shocking result. In his hotel, cheering supporters swarm the narrow hallways as he pushes his way through them, desperately trying to get his campaign manager alone so they can speak privately. The two men succeed in ducking down another hallway and grabbing a few seconds alone in an empty room. As the supporters push their way into that room, too, eager to escort the newly elected senator to the ballroom for the victory speech, Robert Redford's character mouths a question to the campaign manager, a question that the movie does not even attempt to address as the scene fades to black: "What do we do now?"

That's the question I wrote this book to answer.

3

ELVIS AND MIKE TYSON AND ME

There is lots of talk about division and polarization in America: the causes, the trends, the demographics. This talk can be helpful—it's good to know what things are really like and how they got this way. But though that kind of talk can be helpful, it is not sufficient—it doesn't change anything. Instead of talking about division, the more urgent and interesting question to ask is this: How are we going to reach the people on the other side? The people who don't agree with us, don't like us, and in some cases hate us?

Our world is deeply divided. But what should we do about it? How are we going to overcome division and polarization and enmity? I find that there is lots of talk these days about division— theory and analysis and complaint about division—but very little talk about action. Elvis Presley—of all people—captures my sentiments exactly: "A little less conversation, a little more action, please!"

In a divided world, regardless of who you are or to what group or tribe you belong, there will always be other people who do not think like you or agree with you. And, unfortunately, in our divided world there will also be people who dislike you and even hate you. If you don't have a plan to reach those people, you are unlikely to make a difference. It's easy to reach the folks who are on your side, but what will actually change things is reaching the people on the *other* side, and that's much harder. This is because any proposal that hopes to bring real change in our divided world must account for the fact that other people will be devoted to defeating it.

Whether you are a vegan or a West Texas wildcatter, whether you are a Hasidic Jew or a gun owner, whether you are an environmental activist or a religious conservative—and even if you are all of the above—there are millions of other people who want the exact opposite thing from what you want, and millions of people who are working to oppose what you want and implement its opposite. In the words of Mike Tyson, "Everyone has a plan till they get punched in the mouth."[1] What's your plan to reach those people and win them over to your point of view?

Good intentions will not be enough. You can say you want world peace, but unless you have a plan to win over the people who want war, and unless you are willing to back that up with conviction and sacrificial action, your good intentions won't amount to all that much.

Gaining political power and achieving electoral victories can seem like the answer, but political power is by its nature impermanent and incomplete. Even if your party wins at the ballot box, there will still be millions of people who voted against what you voted for, people who will then work hard to overturn whatever the last election made possible. Political victories are usually short-lived. There is always another election in the future, and political popularity tends to swing like a pendulum between opposing parties—who is up will then be down, and vice versa.

No, political power alone will not get us what we want. So how do we motivate deeper change than the changes wrought at the ballot box? How do we change the people on the other side?

Of course, there have always been people throughout

history who decided that reaching their opponents was a fool's errand and that violence was the best way to overcome division—just kill the people in the way. Violence *is* effective, but only in the short term. This is because controlling and coercing other people through violence will constantly require more and more violence just to maintain control, and soon the path of violence will become an all-encompassing end in itself—a police state requires a lot of policing. Are you going to kill *everyone* who stands in the way? And in the end, of course, we cannot actually sidestep the moral question anyway: Each of us will have to stand before the Lord on judgment day, and may God have mercy on the ones who chose to live by the sword. Violence is not the answer.

Whoever we are, we must confront the stone-cold fact that in this country there are millions of people who do not like us or think like us or believe like us—people who want the exact opposite of what we want—and they aren't going anywhere.

For Christians the question of how to reach those who hate us has a particular urgency because Jesus has told us that reaching every single people group on earth is the church's divine purpose: "Go and make disciples of all nations" (Matt. 28:19). In the divided world in which we find ourselves, how are we going to reach the people who do not share our beliefs? What do we do now? Is there any way to break through and reach the people on the other side?

There is, and this book is about how to do it. I am tired of just talking about the problems that divide us, and so this is a book about how to go on offense. I'm writing as a pastor interested in equipping people to take action, to reach across division. This book is about how we, as American Christians, can reach the people who believe *we* are the problem, those who hate us and all we stand for. And though our situation might seem difficult, this book is not a complaint or an indulgent excuse, it is a way forward. Which is good, because with regard to its divine mission of reaching the world, the church is facing an unprecedented challenge.

THE CHURCH'S UNPRECEDENTED PROBLEM

American culture today has an overall rather negative view of Christianity. Whereas in the past it could be helpful if you were known to attend church and profess the Christian faith, in many segments of society today it is not a benefit to be known as a Bible-believing Christian. Christians who hold to traditional Christian beliefs will find themselves largely out of step with elite secular opinions. These cultural headwinds are blowing us farther apart and make reaching others more difficult.

But the harder challenge is this: For the first time in Christian history, the church in the West is faced with the task of evangelizing a post-Christian culture—with the modifier *post* being key. For more than two thousand years, the Christian church in its various divisions and denominations has brought the Good News to untold numbers of tribes, tongues, peoples, and nations who had never heard it. These were all pre-Christian cultures, people who had never before heard the gospel or, in some cases, the name of Jesus Christ. Over and over again these cultures were captured for Christ, and the good news of Jesus transformed one life, one law, one idea at a time. The church knows how to reach people who have never heard about Jesus, and we've been remarkably successful at this task.

But now the church in the West faces an unprecedented mission, that of reevangelizing a formerly Christian culture, a post-Christian culture. Our culture can be considered post-Christian because although Christ's influence is still felt everywhere in the West, those who benefit from his influence and the blessings he has bestowed won't acknowledge they come from him. In fact, our so-called secular values are largely derived from Christian values; ideas and values such as human rights, care for the poor, the dignity of the individual, equality before the law—these ideas and values all have their roots in Christianity. Yet today these values have been cut off from their roots. Like flowers in a florist's display, the beauty of Christianity is still evident in our culture, but our culture has been cut off from its life-giving source. Though Christian values still undergird much of the ethical, legal, and moral framework of Western culture, the culture that benefits from these values has no use for the Christ who gave them or for the church that preached them. The church that shaped Western culture for two millennia is now in the process of being rejected by that same culture. It is certainly nothing new for the church to be hated—Jesus himself warned us to expect opposition—but it *is* unprecedented for the church to be hated by a culture that once used to honor and respect it. *Anti*-Christian is not new, but *post*-Christian is. The church has never been in this kind of cultural moment before, and so we have an unprecedented problem. What do we do now?

WHY THIS IS NOT JUST ANOTHER SELF-HELP BOOK

This is a book about what to do, about how to move forward in our divided and polarized world, about how to change the world. It is based on a simple insight into how the world actually works and how people actually change. I hope the principle I propose will motivate people to decide to move from complaint to action, from being victims to taking agency, and that people who follow this principle (and are willing to pay the price) will overcome division and thereby realize lasting change in both the political and personal spheres. More than that, I am writing this book because I want to offer a way forward for the church in the twenty-first century, and I'm praying that the American church will see a remarkable spiritual harvest by reaching the very people who are most hard-hearted and hateful toward Jesus.

But because the argument of this book is that the way to get big things done is by focusing on the small things, that the way to make big changes is by starting with small interactions, this book could almost fit right in on the self-help shelf. The message of this book is immediately applicable to every relationship in our lives, from the most intimate and significant, such as our spouses and families, to the more transactional and temporary, such as the client we struggle to agree with, the cashier at the grocery store, the next-door neighbor with the political sign in the front yard. I hope marriages will be healed and enemies reconciled because of the contents of this book.

But this is not really just another self-help book. It is actually a book about the love of God. It is a theological reflection on two profound, related ideas:

1. God is love.
2. We love because God first loved us.

And more than changing others, I believe that the central idea of this book has the power to help us change ourselves.

Love goes first. Those three words are a definition and an admonition—they are about what love is and about what love does. This three-word principle is a way to make love practical, and, as I will argue in the book, it is our way forward in a divided and polarized world. "What do we do now?" My answer: If you want to change the world, you have to go first, because love goes first. The rest of this book will explain what that means.

We will start by examining the cultural context in which we find ourselves. What does it mean that we now live in what one writer has called the negative world? By starting here, we will be able to understand why many of our former techniques and tools for evangelization are no longer working as effectively as they once did. Next, we'll look at four possible paths the church could take—three of them will be dead ends, but one of them is the way forward. We'll look at the last book of the Bible, the book of Revelation, to see what has been revealed to the church about the nature of history and God's plan for the church to fulfill the Great Commission. The insight from Jesus to his church revealed through John's vision will help us reject the wrong answers to our central question, What do we do now?

Then we will look at the past several centuries in Western thought and see how, in a culture that supposedly values science and rationality, we have gotten to the point where feelings seem more important than facts for so many people. But, drawing inspiration from my mother's advice for avoiding venomous snakes, the war-fighting doctrine of a maverick fighter pilot, and the basics of a ping-pong match, we will see that, if you want to change the world, you have to go first, because love goes first.

This insight will require us to get clear as to what, exactly, love is. Therefore, we will define love not according to the sentimental definition the world gives but by looking at God himself. We will see how the love of God has gone first from the beginning and how a pattern of love is woven throughout the Bible and in everyday life. There are examples everywhere, involving people as disparate as billionaire owners of football teams, reluctant biblical prophets, crazy-haired Oscar-winning directors, and crooked and diminutive tax collectors with unexpected houseguests. We will look at these and other examples to better understand what it means to say that love goes first.

But love always comes with a cost, and we have to acknowledge and prepare for that cost. Going first might even cost us everything. The good news is that Jesus was raised from the dead, and no actions done in love will ever be a waste. And so we'll end with a brief note of hope: Not only is it possible for us to evangelize this post-Christian culture in which we find ourselves, the Lord is eager to involve us in his plan for doing so, if we'll just listen to and trust him. And so there really is nothing else for it but to get up and go.

As I have said, this is a book about taking action. But to rush in without first surveying the terrain and counting the cost would be foolish. So we will spend the next few chapters trying to understand where we are and how we got here. We'll begin by looking at a Super Bowl commercial and what the reaction to it can tell the church about the times in which we are living.

DISCUSSION QUESTIONS

1. What are some of the ways that people are divided from one another these days?

2. If we all recognize and lament these divisions, why are we still divided? Why are our divisions so difficult to overcome?

3. What was Mike Tyson getting at when he said, "Everyone has a plan till they get punched in the mouth?"

4. Why might someone describe modern American culture as post-Christian? What evidence have you personally seen that supports or refutes this claim?

5. The entire chapter of 1 John 4 is worth reading. It contains

the two statements emphasized above: first, that God is love, and second, that we love because God first loved us. We will look at these statements in greater detail later, but for now what do you think are the implications of these claims for our lives today?

1

WELCOME TO THE NEGATIVE WORLD

American culture has changed over the past several decades from having a positive view of Christianity to having a negative view of Christianity, and if the church is going to be faithful to its mission, our strategies for reaching people for Jesus will have to change, too.

Then Jesus came to them and said, "All authority in heaven and on earth has been given to me. Therefore go and make disciples of all nations, baptizing them in the name of the Father and of the Son and of the Holy Spirit, and teaching them to obey everything I have commanded you. And surely I am with you always, to the very end of the age."
—MATTHEW 28:18–20

On February 12, 2023, a group called He Gets Us ran two commercials during that year's Super Bowl telecast. The Super Bowl draws in millions of American viewers, and though thirty seconds of airtime costs a fortune, if you want to reach America, running a commercial during the NFL's big game is the way to do it. He Gets Us is a Christian marketing group that wants people to give Jesus another look. It is trying to reach people who neither go to church nor have a relationship with Jesus. And what better way to get people to give Jesus a second look than to get their attention during the Super Bowl?

The two commercials He Gets Us ran that evening looked like the other commercials on the telecast, but their message was unlike anything else viewers saw during the game. I remember seeing the second of the two ads live and being moved by both the message and the brilliance of the advertising pitch. Over a soundtrack with a thumping bass line, the ad—titled "Love Your Enemies"—showed a series of black-and-white photos of Americans, of every group and tribe, frozen in argument or confrontation, midscream. It was a catalog of recent American divisions and hatred. Then at the culminating moment, the ad went to black and showed a simple message: "Jesus loved the people we hate." That was it.[1]

The ad is brilliant because it makes you think of Jesus in a way that most people haven't—as someone who is reaching out to the very people we don't like. I was moved. The commercial was emotionally affecting and made me consider both Jesus' courage and my need to be transformed to be more like him. I felt convicted in the Christian sense of the term—forced to admit that, instead of loving the people I don't like, I have often allowed myself to be pulled into a rip current of fear and dislike. The ad was a mirror showing me something about myself that I hadn't wanted to see. At the same time, it showed me Jesus in a way that made me love and admire him more—caused me to consider his great personal courage and what it took for him to reach out to the people who hated him. I thought the entire ad was perfect. I loved it.

The media did not.

Over that Super Bowl weekend, I read piece after piece online criticizing the He Gets Us campaign, not because of the ads themselves but because the funders behind the ads are evangelical Christians. To cite one example among many, CNN ran a piece on its website on Super Bowl weekend titled "The Truth Behind the 'He Gets Us' Ads for Jesus Airing During the Super Bowl." Here is an excerpt from that article:

> Certain details about the "He Gets Us" ads have set off alarm bells among young people and those skeptical of religion, two groups the campaign is specifically trying to attract. Some of the campaign's major donors, and its holding company, have ties to conservative political aims and far-right ideologies that appear at odds with the campaign's inclusive messaging. . . .

While donors who support "He Gets Us" can choose to remain anonymous, Hobby Lobby co-founder David Green claims to be a big contributor to the campaign's multi-million-dollar coffers. Hobby Lobby has famously been at the center of several legal controversies, including the support of anti-LGBTQ legislation and a successful years-long legal fight that eventually led to the Supreme Court allowing companies to deny medical coverage for contraception on the basis of religious beliefs.[2]

The reason the media critics hated the ads had nothing to do with the content of the ads—most attacks on the ads ignored the ads' message, because the content was irrelevant to the critique. Rather, as the excerpt from the CNN article shows, the He Gets Us ads were a problem because of the people behind them. David Green and Hobby Lobby became well known in American political circles after Hobby Lobby was involved in a successful lawsuit to protest the mandating of the so-called morning-after pill as a result of the Affordable Care Act signed into law by President Barack Obama. The He Gets Us ads were guilty by association with the wrong kind of people—Christians who dissent from, among other things, the elite secular consensus around sexuality, marriage, and abortion.

The He Gets Us campaign spent millions of dollars on two advertisements that showed Jesus in an unusual, provocative, and attractive light, advertisements that showed that Jesus offers exactly what the world needs, advertisements that were produced with the highest professional values. And this was the result: Everyone who mattered hated them.

Welcome to the negative world.

JESUS AND THE BIG HAIRY
AUDACIOUS GOAL

In his last words before his ascension, Jesus gave his followers a clear mission, marching orders that Christians have come to call the Great Commission: "Then Jesus came to them and said, 'All authority in heaven and on earth has been given to me. Therefore go and make disciples of all nations, baptizing them in the name of the Father and of the Son and of the Holy Spirit, and teaching them to obey everything I have commanded you. And surely I am with you always, to the very end of the age'" (Matt. 28:18–20).

What is immediately clear from his command is that Jesus expects his church to be on the move, to go somewhere and do something. It's all about going on the offensive: Go and make disciples of all nations—and teach them everything Jesus taught.

Evangelization is the term we use for the first part of this command: go and baptize and make disciples.[3] It's the process by which people hear the gospel and accept it; evangelization is telling people about Jesus, leading them to place their trust in him.

This command is absolute: The church is to go *everywhere* and teach *everything*. When Jesus speaks of all nations, he is speaking not of what we might call nation states or countries but of people groups—the underlying Greek word is the same word from which we get our term *ethnic*. So the expanse of the command is breathtaking—the church is to go and train apprentices to Jesus from every single people group on the planet. And for two thousand years that is exactly what the church has been doing; presumably that task will not be complete until the end of history itself. The Great Commission is what business writer Jim Collins would call a BHAG—pronounced *bee hag*—a "Big Hairy Audacious Goal."[4] The BHAG that Jesus gives the church is breathtaking in its scope and piercing in its clarity. There is no wiggle room or gray area—the terms are *all* and *everything*. This BHAG is the church's mission until Jesus returns and history ends. In all times and all places, the church has the same mission: to go and make disciples. That mission never changes. But what happens when culture does?

THINGS HAVE CHANGED

Things are different these days. Over the past decade, American culture has changed in ways that have become more hostile to the church and the claims of Christ. As a result, a majority of those who hold the keys of power in American society—in politics, media, and education—have a negative view of Christianity. In light of these changes, I believe that the most important distinction in the American church today is not between liberal and conservative, high church and low church, mainline and evangelical. No, the most important distinction in the American church today is between those who recognize we live in what one writer has called "the negative world"[5] and those who have not yet accepted this fact.

This distinction matters because it directly affects our strategies for carrying out the Great Commission. Our mission from Jesus has not changed, and our responsibility to evangelize cannot be avoided. But the strategies we employ to complete that mission need to be constantly shifting, depending on the cultural context. The problem we face today is that many of our strategies for evangelism were developed in and for a previous cultural context, one that was largely positive about Christianity and that saw the Christian faith as either something good or at best neutral. But that culture is gone, and it's time for new strategies. If we keep running our plays out of the old playbook, we are going to lose the game.

In prior times in American history, the church's strategy for evangelization was to call people back to the faith they knew to be true. In those times, American culture was largely shaped by Christian values and teachings (though of course not everyone was a devout Christian and American society was far from perfect, as the existence of slavery and segregation—among other things—shows), and the goal of pastors and evangelists was to encourage people to return to the fold. In those days the institutions and organs of society—politics, finance, education, and so on—generally supported the teachings of the church. In our day that is no longer the case, and our primary strategy for evangelization cannot be to call people back to faith because many people have never known the Christian faith to begin with. Rather, the question we need to ask is far more pointed and direct: How are we going to reach the people who hate us? There is a growing suspicion among many today that Christianity is not just misguided and wrong but is the source of many of our problems. Times have changed, and we need to get with the times.

The high point of church attendance in America was in the years immediately following the Second World War: About half of the American population attended church weekly in the 1950s, which was a higher percentage than in any other period in American history.[6] Church attendance in America peaked in the postwar years, and it has been falling ever since. By the time the late 1960s arrived, it was obvious to everyone that American culture was changing, and those changes continued over subsequent decades.

Aaron Renn studied these changes and, drawing on his training as a management consultant, wrote a book called *Life in the Negative World*, in which he proposes a simple framework we can use to better understand the contemporary church and its relationship to American culture. He suggests that we look at postwar American culture as being divided into three phases. The key issue in each phase is whether being a Christian increases or decreases one's social capital. Is being known as a follower of Christ positive, neutral, or negative? Will being a Christian win you friends and help you influence people, help you get a job, and garner you social approval? Or will it attract scorn and opposition? Renn calls these three phases the positive world, the neutral world, and the negative world. His proposal is known commonly as the three-worlds framework, and I believe it is helpful in showing us that things really are different these days—we're not dreaming—and, more important, why the ways we used to evangelize will no longer be as effective as they once were.

THE POSITIVE WORLD

Renn dates the positive world for Christianity in America from roughly 1964 to 1994. In positive-world Christianity, church attendance patterns had already peaked and American culture had begun to shift, but, in general, it was considered a social good if you were known as an upstanding Christian. You might be the president of your bank and known for serving on the board of your church and most everyone would think those were good things. It was an advantage in business and politics to be associated with the church. In the positive world, American culture still basically accepted the claims of the faith, and the culture was positively disposed toward Christianity.

Here's a pop-culture example that illustrates what the positive world was like (and it also shows us how much things have changed). In December 1965 the well-known TV special *A Charlie Brown Christmas* aired on CBS. Throughout the program, Charlie Brown asks his friends about the true meaning of Christmas. In the climactic scene, Charlie's friend Linus decides to give us the definitive answer, so he takes center stage at the school play and recites the Christmas story from the gospel of Luke.

> And there were in the same country shepherds abiding in the field, keeping watch over their flock by night. And, lo, the angel of the Lord came upon them, and the glory of the Lord shone round about them: and they were sore afraid. And the angel said unto them, Fear not: for, behold, I bring you good tidings of great joy, which shall be to all people. For unto you is born this day in the city of David a Saviour, which is Christ the Lord. And this shall be a sign unto you; Ye shall find the babe wrapped in swaddling clothes, lying in a manger. And suddenly there was with the angel a multitude of the heavenly host praising God, and saying, Glory to God in the highest, and on earth peace, good will toward men.
>
> —LUKE 2:8–14 KJV

The famous Charlie Brown soundtrack drops out, and Linus walks off the middle of the stage in silence. He approaches Charlie Brown and says, "That's what Christmas is all about, Charlie Brown." It's a stunning scene, and anyone who watches it now immediately thinks, "There is no way they would make that today." Exactly.

It was a different time, and the church occupied a place in American society different from where it stands today. It also had evangelistic strategies fit for those times. Consider the strategies for evangelism used by Billy Graham in his famous crusades. Graham would buy out large arenas and persuade people through his preaching that they needed to accept Christ or face eternal judgment. His ministry was effective at reaching the lost because they knew they were lost. In the positive world even those who were not devout or baptized accepted the terms outlined by the Christian story—the notion that there is objective good and evil and that people are in some way accountable to God, their creator. In that culture at that time, it was good, acceptable, and even expected that you might be a Christian, and the institutions of society implicitly supported the church in conveying that expectation. An evangelist such as Billy Graham could use the cultural Christianity of his listeners to his advantage by calling people to repent and come back to faith.

In *Unbroken*, her bestselling account of the remarkable life of Olympian and World War II prisoner of war Louis Zamperini, author Laura Hillenbrand recounts the circumstances of Louie's conversion at the Reverend Billy Graham's first major crusade, which took place in Los Angeles for eight weeks in the fall of 1949. In doing so, she provides a helpful example of the evangelistic strategy Billy Graham would use over the years to great effect. Louie had been an Olympic runner, then survived a plane crash in the Pacific Ocean during the war, and was subsequently a prisoner of war of the Japanese— during the years of his imprisonment he was tortured and tormented. When he was finally liberated at the end of the war, he was a broken man and sank into drinking and despair. By 1949 his marriage was dead, and in desperation his wife begged him to attend the revival services Billy Graham was holding each night in a tent on an empty lot in downtown Los Angeles. Reluctantly, Louie finally agreed. After they arrived, Graham began to preach from John chapter 8, the story of the woman caught in the act of adultery.

Louie was suddenly wide awake. Describing Jesus rising from his knees after a night of prayer, Graham asked his listeners how long it had been since they'd prayed in earnest. Then he focused on Jesus bending down, his finger tracing words in the sand at the Pharisees' feet, sending the men scattering in fear.

"What did they see Jesus write?" Graham asked. Inside himself, Louie felt something twisting.

"Darkness doesn't hide the eyes of God," Graham said. "God takes down your life from the time you were born to the time you die. And when you stand before God on the great judgment day, you're going to say, 'Lord I wasn't such a bad fellow,' and they are going to pull down the screen and they are going to shoot the moving picture of your life from the cradle to the grave, and you are going to hear every thought that was going through your mind every minute of the day, every second of the minute, and you're going to hear the words that you said. And your own words, and your own thoughts, and your own deeds are going to condemn you as you stand before God on that day. And God is going to say, 'Depart from me.'"

Louie felt indignant rage flaring in him, a struck match. *I am a good man*, he thought. *I am a good man*.

27

Even as he had this thought, he felt the lie in it. He knew what he had become. Somewhere under his anger, there was a lurking, nameless uneasiness, the shudder of sharks rasping their backs along the bottom of the raft. There was a thought he must not think, a memory he must not see. With the urgency of a bolting animal, he wanted to run.[7]

Louie left the tent that night stubbornly unconverted, but he returned the following evening and decided to accept the altar-call invitation that Graham offered and give his life to Christ. It is a moving account of a turning point in a remarkable life.

What is particularly relevant in our case is the question that Billy Graham put to his audience that evening in 1949: "Graham asked his listeners how long it had been since they'd prayed in earnest." His question presumed that ordinary Americans knew that they were supposed to pray and—this is a crucial insight—it presumed that at some point previously these ordinary Americans had actually prayed. Note that the question was meant to call people back to what they knew to be true. And the passage in his sermon about standing before God on judgment day was meant to cause the listeners to admit—at least to themselves—that they were sinners who knew they had fallen short of God's standards.

In the positive world, effective evangelism reminded people what they knew in their bones to be true: that sin is bad, that they were sinners, and that they needed the grace of God. These were messages the wider culture tacitly taught, and it meant a child growing up in this period learned them without even really knowing he or she was learning them. Though Louis Zamperini's conversion took place in 1949—before the positive world begins in Aaron Renn's three-worlds framework—the basic evangelistic strategy of the positive world was not all that different from those of the eras before it. The evangelistic strategy of the American church was effectively unchanged since the days of Jonathan Edwards and colonial America. That strategy had largely consisted of preachers calling people back to faith—people were told that they had fallen away, that there was penalty for sin, and that they were in need of grace. It was time to come back and give their lives to the Lord.

But what happens when people no longer believe those things?

THE NEUTRAL WORLD

In Aaron Renn's three-worlds framework, after the positive world comes the neutral world, which Renn dates from roughly 1994 to 2014. In the neutral world, the Christian faith is one option among many. Imagine a cafeteria of belief systems in which you can pick out what beliefs seem most appetizing to you. You can follow Jesus or you can take up your mat and follow the practices of yoga. Christianity is seen no longer as the preeminent set of values in America but rather as a values set that works for some people and not for others. The broader culture is not opposed to Christianity but rather has a neutral disposition toward Christianity, which it sees as one option among many.

In the neutral world, people were no longer inclined to accept at face value the church's claims as personally binding and universally true, but they were still willing to hear them out. In the neutral world, therefore, effective evangelization started with getting a hearing for the gospel. This meant that churches employed attractional ministry strategies that emphasized how Jesus also cared about the things secular culture cared about. Many churches in the neutral world showcased their commitment to the arts or to social justice or to community gardens as a way of attracting interested nonbelievers, with the expectation that those interested people would then hear the gospel at a church event and follow Jesus. In the neutral world, it was no longer an obvious social good for the bank president to be the president of the men's group at his church, but neither was it a significant liability. As long as the bank president did not force his beliefs on his colleagues, then his being a Christian was not any different from his colleague being a triathlete or his client being a libertarian. These were all equally valid ways of living, equally appropriate lifestyle choices for a person to make.

In the neutral world, the church could no longer simply call people to repentance and expect a large response, because people were not convinced that they needed to repent, nor were they as interested in listening to what the church had to say just because it was the church. Though the message was the same—"Repent and believe the gospel"—in the neutral world churches had to experiment with different ways of getting people's attention. Because Christianity was just one option among many, you had to work to get your foot in the door before people were

willing to give you a hearing. Think of the attractional practices that so many American megachurches used in the early
years of the twenty-first century—over-the-top Christmas
productions and celebrity speakers and climbing walls in the
high-school-ministry buildings. These and other practices
were intended to get people in the door so they would then
hear the gospel. If Christianity is one option among many, then
you must do whatever it takes to get people to at least consider
giving Jesus a chance.[*]

But what happens when Christianity goes from being one
option among many possible options to something socially
unwelcome and problematic?

Welcome to the negative world.

THE NEGATIVE WORLD

Aaron Renn dates the start of the negative world to sometime
around 2014. In the negative world, Christianity is no longer
seen as a positive good for society, as in the positive world,
and neither is it one acceptable option among many options,
as in the neutral world. No, in the negative world, being a
Christian—or at least being the wrong kind of Christian—is
a social negative.

---

[*] In the neutral world, there were times and places when an attractional strategy
was effective in bringing people to faith. My point here is not to critique these
practices but merely to point out the cultural period in which they were developed
and in which they were effective: the neutral world.

What is the wrong kind of Christian? The *wrong kind of Christian* is a tongue-in-cheek term I use to be provocative, and it describes one who dissents—however politely—from the negative-world cultural consensus:

- If you do not accept the claim that all religions essentially lead to the same truth, then you are the wrong type of Christian.
- If you do not believe that everyone creates his or her own truth, and that truth is whatever best works for a person, then you are the wrong type of Christian.
- If you do not believe that the human body has no inherent meaning and that we are essentially defined by our sexual desires, and that no type of consenting sexual activity can ever be morally wrong, then you are the wrong type of Christian.
- If you do not believe that proselytization is wrong (unless you are trying to convert people away from Christianity), then you are the wrong type of Christian.

In the negative world it is possible to be a Christian and hold an influential position in secular society, but it is much easier if you are the "right kind of Christian"—one who goes along with whatever secular culture declares to be good and true. To be the wrong kind of Christian and work in a high-profile position in Washington or Wall Street or Hollywood is difficult. If you are known as the wrong type of Christian, it is more likely than not that your faith will negatively affect your career possibilities.

Here are two examples from politics that roughly correspond to the neutral-world and negative-world timelines and help illustrate the change.

In January 2009 there was some controversy when Rick Warren, pastor of Saddleback Church in California, was invited to pray at the presidential inauguration of Barack Obama.[8] Rick Warren is an evangelical and was known for teaching traditional Christian sexual ethics as well as opposing abortion. Despite some complaints when word got out that Mr. Warren had been invited to pray, the Obama inaugural team did not rescind its invitation to Warren, who gave a standard Christian prayer at the inauguration.

Fast-forward four years. In January 2013 Pastor Louie Giglio of Passion City Church in Atlanta was invited by the Obama team to pray at President Obama's second inauguration. After that announcement was made, activists publicized a sermon that Mr. Giglio preached in the 1990s in which he spoke out against same-sex sexual activity. After that sermon was made public, Giglio withdrew from the event. A spokesperson for the Obama team said, "We were not aware of Pastor Giglio's past comments at the time of his selection and they don't reflect our desire to celebrate the strength and diversity of our country at this Inaugural."[9]

Let us compare the two incidents. In January 2009, Rick Warren—arguably one of the most well-known pastors in America—prayed at that year's presidential inauguration, even though he had been recently on the record supporting traditional marriage. (In the fall of 2008 he had spoken in favor of the California referendum that would ban gay marriage.) Though there was some pushback from pro-same-sex-marriage groups against his inclusion, the event went forward with him in attendance. Yet four years later, in January 2013, Louie Giglio—a less well-known pastor—was gracelessly disinvited from that year's presidential inauguration because of a sermon he had preached twenty years before. The differing responses illustrate the change in America as the neutral world gave way to the negative world. When he was running for the Senate in 2004, Barack Obama himself famously said that he believed "marriage is something sanctified between a man and a woman."[10] Yet by his second presidential term, he had "evolved" and had become a supporter of same-sex marriage.[11] In the neutral world, a politician needed to reflect a more neutral view of same-sex marriage if he wanted to be elected to the presidency. As the neutral world gave way to the negative world, however, it was to a politician's benefit to be known as a supporter of same-sex marriage, even though such a position was a major break with historic Christian teaching on the subject. In the negative world it is very difficult to win elections without at least tacitly endorsing the sexual revolution. Historic Christian teaching—at least in places where it conflicts with the new cultural consensus—is no longer a positive push but has become a negative pull on career success.

NEGATIVELY NARROW IN ONE WAY ONLY

Someone might raise one of the following objections to this negative-world analysis:

- How can you call our current time the negative world when for so many centuries black American Christians faced slavery and segregation? Were not things much more negative then?
- How can American Christians talk about the negative world while Christians in other parts of the world are facing violent persecution?
- Jesus told his followers to expect to be hated, and the early Christians faced martyrdom, so a little opposition is nothing new.

These are all true statements. But they miss the nuanced point Renn is making with his framework. To call our cultural moment the negative world is not to suggest that things are somehow worse today than they have ever been. Nor is it to say that Christians in America have it worse than believers in other parts of the world. As these objections point out, not too long ago in America we had slavery and then segregation, and it is no secret that in other parts of the world today Christians face daily threats of persecution and death. To say that this cultural moment is the negative world is not to say anything about the experiences of Christian minorities or the persecuted church around the world, now or in the past. Yes, there are still subcultures in America in which being known as a Christian can be an asset to career advancement. Yes, there is much we can learn from the black church's long experience of living in difficult cultural and legal circumstances in America. And yes, there have always been Christians who were persecuted for their beliefs. No one is denying any of this. Our cultural moment can be labeled "negative world" for one simple, narrow reason: When we consider our culture more generally, and in particular those institutions that shape culture—especially the media and higher education—Christianity is no longer seen as a cultural asset or a social good but rather seen as something negative, and this is a change from our recent past. Traditional Christian beliefs are now seen in many quarters as problematic or evil, and publicly identifying yourself as a Christian who holds these beliefs will likely hurt your chances of success in many social environments today—thus, "negative world."

To say we are living in the negative world is not to whine or claim some kind of victim status. (We shall see that the way forward for the church will involve our explicit rejection of the victim mentality.) The point of concluding that we are living in the negative world is just to cause us to examine our strategies for evangelism. Are they a good fit for these times? A strategy for evangelism that calls people back to faith will not be effective in the negative world because that strategy wrongly assumes that people know the truth but have not been living by it, and that they know that they should be living by it. Yet today many people no longer accept the truth claims of the Christian faith, and the declining rates of church attendance in America bear this out. If you were to pick out a random person in Times Square and ask, "Do you believe you are a sinner?" that person may not even understand what you mean or is just as likely to reply, "I'm a pretty good person and I don't believe in a judgmental God." Because people no longer accept at face value the church's truth claims, they are not particularly inclined to give the gospel message a hearing. The strategies for evangelism the church has used in the recent past will therefore not be as effective in the negative world.

At this point you might object, "It doesn't matter what someone thinks about the gospel, what matters is the truth." I agree. Whether we live in positive, neutral, negative, or Disney World, the tomb is still empty and Jesus still reigns. Truth is truth. The church's mission from Jesus has not changed. The Great Commission still applies, and we are commanded to go everywhere and make disciples. The mission has not changed, but the strategies we employ to accomplish that mission will vary depending on the time and place and circumstances. The message is the same, but how we share the message will be different depending on whether the person to whom we're speaking lives in inner-city New York or rural Alabama, or is part of an unreached people group in Indonesia. What do you do when strategies developed for another culture no longer work in the current culture? What do we do now?

I'm convinced that Aaron Renn is right: We live in the negative world. When we look out at our divided, polarized world, we need accept that because American culture has changed, the evangelism strategies that the church developed in a previous time will no longer be as effective in our time. Accepting that fact is the first step to actually making a difference and taking action. But before we can take action, we need to be sure we are taking the right action. To jump into action without first evaluating all the options before us is foolish. In my view, there are four possible options in front of us. We'll look at each of the four in turn and we'll conclude that only one will actually take us where we want to go.

DISCUSSION QUESTIONS

1. The author remarked that the He Gets Us ad made him think of Jesus as courageous. Have you ever thought of Jesus showing courage, and if so, what made you think that?

2. Have you felt yourself being pulled into "a rip current of fear and dislike"? What did you have to do to break free?

3. Do you agree that American culture has grown more hostile to the claims of Christ? In what ways have you seen this happening?

4. Think about the word *sin*. Is sin a real thing to people today?

5. Are there Christian beliefs you espouse that you are reluctant to publicly share?

6. What does it mean to say that we are living in the negative world? Does this designation mean that previous periods in American history were perfect?

THREE DEAD ENDS, ONE WAY FORWARD

In the negative world, the church could choose accommodation, judgment, or withdrawal, but to go down any of those paths will lead us to the same dead end. Fortunately, there is another option.

"**You are the salt of the earth, but if salt has lost its taste, how shall its saltiness be restored? It is no longer good for anything except to be thrown out and trampled under people's feet.**
"**You are the light of the world. A city set on a hill cannot be hidden. Nor do people light a lamp and put it under a basket, but on a stand, and it gives light to all in the house. In the same way, let your light shine before others, so that they may see your good works and give glory to your Father who is in heaven.**"
—MATTHEW 5:13–16 ESV

Masada is an absolutely staggering sight. Located in modern Israel, it is a magnificent stone fortress that stands in the Judean desert not far from the Dead Sea. Built by Herod the Great in the thirties BC, even two thousand years later it is breathtaking in its audacity. Located in one of the driest and harshest climates in the world, it lies on a flat isolated clifftop and features steep drops on every side. The very fact it was built at all is proof of King Herod's ambition and ruthless exercise of raw power. All water and food had to be brought up the cliff, and when supplied, the fortress was virtually impregnable.

The temple that Herod built in Jerusalem—the same temple in which Jesus walked—was destroyed by the Romans in AD 70 in the midst of the First Jewish Revolt. The rebels then fled to the desert and took up positions in Masada and prepared for a siege. The Romans obliged and Masada was besieged from AD 72 to 73. The way the Romans ultimately defeated the Jewish freedom fighters is almost as astounding as Masada itself: They spent years building a huge siege ramp that allowed them to walk right up to the clifftop fortress—hundreds of feet in the air—and then used a battering ram to break through its walls. When the Romans finally entered the citadel, they found that the remaining Jewish defenders had all committed suicide rather than be captured by their hated oppressors.[1]

There are four options facing the church as it seeks to move forward in the negative world, but three of those options are dead ends. Like the fortress at Masada, the first three options we will consider might seem to provide strength and security, but if we take them, there will be only one outcome: death for the church.

POST-CHRISTIAN

In the previous chapter, we looked at what it means that our culture now has a negative view of Christianity. Another way of making the same point is to say that, for the first time in American history, we are living in a post-Christian society. What happens when a flower is cut off from its roots? What do we do now? Let us consider some of the aspects of this post-Christian culture in which we find ourselves, so we can appropriately understand the challenges we face if we want to reach this culture for Christ.

The fish does not know that it's wet, and to us in the modern world our beliefs seem self-evident. We take them for granted. "Of course this is true." But people living in the ancient world would see as absurd and preposterous much of what we see as self-evident and obvious. For example, the idea that every single person has value, or that humility is an admirable quality, or that mercy toward someone in a position of weakness is beautiful, or that women and the poor are just as inherently precious as men and the wealthy, that the rich have an obligation to the poor, that a human being is possessed of inalienable human rights—all of these ideas would have been laughable, and even crazy, to people in the ancient world, and all of these ideas came out of the church. Since that first Easter Sunday, the church has claimed that Jesus is lord of the world, and the implications of that claim resulted in what one recent historian has called a revolution.[2] This Christian revolution was a moral revolution, and it has led to human flourishing on a vast and unprecedented scale. It is no exaggeration to say that wherever Christianity has spread, it has improved the lives of the people it has reached.

Versions of this argument are not new. More than one hundred years ago, the philosopher Friedrich Nietzsche argued against Christianity by saying that—in contrast to the pagan societies that preceded it—the Christian faith had made weakness a virtue. More recently the historian Tom Holland has made a related argument in a more positive way in his bestselling book *Dominion*: that what modern people take to be good and true are values that came out of the church, values that no pagan in ancient Rome would have espoused. The ideas and values that modern secular people hold dear are rooted in the sacred beliefs of the Christian church.

The problem we face today is that our culture wants to retain some of those values but no longer has much use for the church that birthed them. This is one way of understanding what it means that we live in a post-Christian culture. Our world is post-Christian in a specific way: Though our society was built on the belief that Jesus Christ is Lord, it no longer affirms that belief. On the contrary, modern Western culture—or at least the culture makers and opinion shapers in elite positions—has come to reject the uniqueness of Jesus and the truth claims of his church. American culture thus finds itself in the strange situation of living in a house someone else built, enjoying its sturdy construction, its attractive design, its livable layout, and its firm foundation, but hating both the builders who built it and many of the "problematic" beliefs they espoused.

These are just a few indications of what it means when we say that modern Western culture is post-Christian. It is a culture still shaped to some extent by Christian values, but it is also a culture that wants to pick and choose, rejecting the church that preached these beliefs and the Christ who gave them. This puts the church in an unprecedented cultural moment.

In light of the fact that American culture has a negative view of Christianity, how should the church proceed? I believe there are three tempting options before us: We can embrace accommodation, we can proclaim judgment, or we can withdraw from the culture and hope it ignores us. Each of these options is tempting because it seems to provide a way forward that acknowledges the difficulty of evangelism in a post-Christian culture. But as we shall see, each of these three options is a dead end and none of them is faithful, because they do not enable us to do what Jesus told us to do.

DEAD END 1: ACCOMMODATION

Faced with the challenge of evangelizing in the negative world, the church could decide to accommodate, blend in, give up, give in. We could let go of anything that makes us distinct—including the exclusive claims of Christ—and become conformed to the pattern of this world. We could decide that we prefer to be the kind of salt that has lost its saltiness. We could choose to sue for peace with hat in hand, begging the enemies of Christ to take us in and promise to be on our best behavior—as they define it. And let's be honest with ourselves: If we go the route of accommodation, we might not have to explicitly renounce Christ so much as simply pretend that Christ's values perfectly align with the world's values. In the negative world, it's the wrong kind of Christian who gets thrown to the lions. The right type of Christian, one willing to go along to get along and agree that there are many different ways to God—that right type of Christian would be applauded. If we want the approval of the powers that be, all we have to do is let go of the beliefs they deem offensive. Accommodation is relatively easy, sort of like freezing to death. You basically do nothing. You simply let the cultural tide sweep you out to sea. Accommodation is the easiest option before us. "Just let go. The tide will do all the work."

Accommodation seems like a prudent option, too. After all, as external pressure increases on the church, it is certainly tempting to go along to get along. What value would the church's martyrdom provide to the world, anyway? What good is persecution? Wouldn't it be better if we quietly made peace with the world and worked for Christ undercover? I can serve Jesus better alive than dead. If I am in a position of influence in my community or company, surely I can do more for Christ by keeping my head down and avoiding trouble than by becoming a lightning rod for soft persecution. How would my family benefit if I took a stand? I'd lose my job and have trouble putting food on the table. What does it profit a man to gain his soul but lose his job?

The temptation to accommodate is strong, and it is understandable. It explains why so many followers of Jesus, when they rise to high positions, turn tame. Over and over again people in positions of influence, whether in media or medicine, in journalism or the executive suite, when faced with a conflict between the world and their commitment to Christ decide to accommodate with the world and let go of Christ. Most of the time they would never admit this is what they have done—we dress up our compromises in ways that save face—but this is what happens nonetheless. We justify our accommodationist stance with the quite reasonable argument that God has raised us to a position for a purpose, and that it would be poor stewardship and a sign of ingratitude to throw it all away by taking a stand. When the temptation to accommodate is particularly strong, we are tempted to imagine ourselves to be an American version of Oskar Schindler, the Nazi industrialist who saved Jews from inside the Third Reich. From the position he held, Schindler was able to do more good than he could have done had he denounced Hitler and lost everything. And while this is undoubtedly true, it raises a question: What about all the other people of good intentions who went along to get along with the Nazis and then, slowly but surely, found themselves participating in horrendous evil and murder? Prudence is a virtue, and it is true that there is no value in seeking out martyrdom for martyrdom's sake. But what about when martyrdom comes to you? Should our goal always be to climb as high as possible and then make accommodations to remain there, justifying our compromises with the idea that the Lord needs us in our lofty positions?

When we are tempted to accommodate out of a concern that taking a stand will undermine what the Lord has done in raising us up, it is good to remember the example of Daniel. Daniel was a Jew living in exile in a foreign land who was raised to prominence in Babylon. But when faced with the choice between remaining faithful to the Lord and staying in favor with the ruling regimes to keep his high position, Daniel chose to be faithful.

In Daniel 6, King Darius issues a written decree declaring that the only form of permissible prayer in his kingdom are prayers directed to the king, and that anyone who violates this decree will be thrown into the lions' den. With death as the punishment for illegal prayer, you might think that Daniel would decide to pray in secret so as not to draw attention to himself. Instead, Daniel does the opposite: "Now when Daniel learned that the decree had been published, he went home to his upstairs room where the windows opened toward Jerusalem. Three times a day he got down on his knees and prayed, giving thanks to his God, just as he had done before" (Dan. 6:10).

Despite the temptation to accommodate the decree of King Darius, Daniel remains faithful and prays with the windows open, with the result being that passersby can see that Daniel is disobeying the king, an action punishable by death. Daniel is subsequently seized and thrown to the lions. The Lord ultimately delivers Daniel from the lions, but Daniel seems to understand that even if the Lord should not deliver him, what makes him valuable to the Lord—and the reason the Lord has raised him to prominence and influence in foreign lands—*is* his faithfulness. Daniel's high position is worthless unless he remains faithful. God doesn't need men of influence; God needs men of faith whom he can raise to positions of influence. Accommodation—going along to get along—is not what the Lord needs from us. God can raise up and pull down: Our task is to avoid taking upon ourselves the burden of making utilitarian calculations—"If I do this, then that will happen, and is that what the Lord wants for me?"—and instead choose, as Daniel did, simply to be faithful.

More important, accommodation would be the death of the church. There is no future for an accommodationist church. Accommodation is spiritual death, a form of dying before we are dead because we no longer have anything to offer the world. While the world might approve of an accommodationist church, we would have nothing life-giving to offer it in return. Young people interviewed on the street might applaud our accommodationist values, but they would never come to our churches. Why seek out what you already have? What would an accommodationist church have to give to the world that the world did not already possess?

Jesus warns us against accommodation in his well-known remarks about salt in the Sermon on the Mount: "You are the salt of the earth. But if the salt loses its saltiness, how can it be made salty again? It is no longer good for anything, except to be thrown out and trampled underfoot" (Matt. 5:13).

Salt has two uses in the kitchen: It enhances, brings out

flavor; and it preserves, keeps things from rotting. Jesus tells his followers that they are like salt: They are to make society better, and they are to keep society from going bad. But what if the church loses its saltiness? What if it loses what makes it distinct? Well, Jesus says that "it is no longer good for anything, except to be thrown out and trampled underfoot."

We can all cite multiple examples over the past two thousand years when the church abandoned what made it distinct and went along with the wider culture. When the church loses its saltiness, the result is always disaster and ruin, for both the church and the world.

If people already have what you are selling, they are not going to buy it. An accommodationist church can give the world only what the world already has. Yet the one thing the world needs and does not have is Jesus. If we let go of him, we are letting go of the only thing that we have worth sharing with the world. We are fools if we believe that if we just ape the world, nonbelievers will beat down our doors to be baptized. A church with no meaningful distinction between itself and the world is a church headed for extinction, inoffensive but irrelevant.

But the most important reason why we should not embrace accommodation is because Jesus specifically warns us against it.

THE APOCALYPSE AND US

Apocalypse is a Greek word that means "uncovering" or "disclosure" or "revealing," from which we get our English word *revelation*. Two thousand years ago, near the end of the first century, a man named John was on the Mediterranean island of Patmos when one Sunday he received an apocalyptic vision that he later wrote down and circulated among the churches of the wealthy Roman province of Asia (the western part of modern-day Turkey). The book of Revelation is that letter.

What many modern readers overlook is the *revelatory* nature of Revelation—the fact that in Revelation we are hearing a message to the church from Jesus himself. In the modern Christian mind, Revelation seems relevant because of what it has to say about the end times, and Revelation does in fact provide insight into how history will come to an end. But by focusing on what Revelation has to tell us about the end, we miss the main point of the vision: that Jesus has a message to share with his church about its role in God's plan now, before the end arrives. To be more specific, the message of Jesus to his church provides a direct answer to our question, What do we do now? And his message can help us avoid false choices and spiritual dead ends as we seek to answer that question.

One of the options before us is accommodation. We've seen why accommodation is guaranteed to fail sociologically: Because an accommodationist church is exactly like the world, it has nothing to offer the world and thus the world will have no interest in it. What Revelation tells us is that accommodation also has no future theologically. Jesus, lord of the church, specifically warns us against it.

Apparently accommodation was just as much a temptation for parts of the church in the first-century Greco-Roman world as it is for us in the twenty-first-century negative world. The entire text of Revelation is a circular letter that was meant to be shared among seven key churches located in separate cities in the Roman province of Asia. But at the beginning of John's vision, Jesus gives a specific message to each of the seven churches in turn. (Imagine Jesus writing a brief note at the top of the letter to each addressee.) There is a recurring theme in the messages that Jesus gives John to give to the churches, a warning against accommodation and compromise with the surrounding culture.

We cannot accommodate even if the pressure to knuckle under increases. Accommodation might look like winning—when you accommodate, you can avoid pressure and persecution—but accommodation would actually mean failure from the point of view of the only person whose opinion ultimately matters: Jesus, lord of the world.

The seventh and final letter, in the beginning chapters of Revelation, is addressed to the church in Laodicea, and it drives home the point that an accommodationist church is repellent to the Lord.

To the Church in Laodicea

"And to the angel of the church in Laodicea write: 'The words of the Amen, the faithful and true witness, the beginning of God's creation.

"'I know your works: you are neither cold nor hot. Would that you were either cold or hot! So, because you are lukewarm, and neither hot nor cold, I will spit you out of my mouth. For you say, I am rich, I have prospered, and I need nothing, not realizing that you are wretched, pitiable, poor, blind, and naked. I counsel you to buy from me gold refined by fire, so that you may be rich, and white garments so that you may clothe yourself and the shame of your nakedness may not be seen, and salve to anoint your eyes, so that you may see. Those whom I love, I reprove and discipline, so be zealous and repent. Behold, I stand at the door and knock. If anyone hears my voice and opens the door, I will come in to him and eat with him, and he with me. The one who conquers, I will grant him to sit with me on my throne, as I also conquered and sat down with my Father on his throne. He who has an ear, let him hear what the Spirit says to the churches.'"

—REVELATION 3:14–22 ESV

To understand the metaphor, we need some cultural context about ancient Laodicea: It was a city without water. As Craig Keener points out,

Laodicea lacked its own water supply, having no direct access to the cold water of the mountains or the hot water of the nearby springs in Hierapolis to the north. In contrast to its claims of self-sufficiency (3:17), it had to pipe in its water. . . . This water had grown lukewarm by the time of its arrival.

The point of lukewarm water is simply that it is disgusting. . . .

Jesus thus finds the church in Laodicea to be other than what he desires. In today's English, he is telling the self-satisfied church in Laodicea: "I want water that will refresh me, but you remind me instead of the water you always complain about. You make me want to puke."[3]

Jesus makes it clear that he wants his church to stand out from the world and to stand firm in its commitment to him. A waffling accommodationist church is repellent to Jesus. What Jesus says to the church in Laodicea is just a vivid restating of his closing message in the Sermon on the Mount: "Not everyone who says to me, 'Lord, Lord,' will enter the kingdom of heaven, but only the one who does the will of my Father who is in heaven. Many will say to me on that day, 'Lord, Lord, did we not prophesy in your name and in your name drive out demons and in your name perform many miracles?' Then I will tell them plainly, 'I never knew you. Away from me, you evildoers!'" (Matt. 7:21–23).

The point in both of these passages is that obedience is a necessary aspect of being a Christian, and there are severe consequences for those who compromise: They have no future with Jesus but will be cast away from his presence.

This is a harsh word, but a sobering one we need to take to heart. This is because in his message to the Laodicean church, Jesus makes an important promise—the future victory of the faithful church: "The one who conquers, I will grant him to sit with me on my throne, as I also conquered and sat down with my Father on his throne" (Rev. 3:21 ESV). Again and again, what Revelation teaches is that the way the church wins is through its steadfast commitment to Jesus, even unto death. For example, in a passage that describes how God's people have achieved victory over their adversary, John hears a voice from heaven shout:

"They triumphed over him
by the blood of the Lamb
and by the word of their testimony;
they did not love their lives so much
as to shrink from death."

—REVELATION 12:11

If the church accommodates and gives in, it will end up letting go of the very means by which it achieves victory— commitment to Jesus.

Accommodation is the first and most obvious temptation we all face, and it is a temptation Jesus addresses. The opening letters to the seven churches in John's vision make it clear that accommodation is abhorrent to Jesus and is not an option for the faithful church. Those who accommodate the prevailing culture face the Lord's judgment and lose their place in his future. It is hard to stand strong and refuse to give in, but it will be much harder for us to stand before the Lord on the day of judgment if we refuse to stand up for him now. God keep us from such a fate.

Accommodation is a dead end.

DEAD END 2: JUDGMENT

The second option we might consider as a strategy for evangelization is the opposite of accommodation: judgment. In a godless culture it could be the case that our primary task is to pronounce judgment on that culture by calling out sin and naming what is abhorrent to God. If our efforts do not seem to be effecting change, then we just need to make more noise. Perhaps the church has been too quiet and accommodating. The solution, therefore, is to get louder. By shouting more forcefully at the unbelieving world, people would finally understand that they are sinners in the hands of an angry God and in desperation they would turn to us and ask, as the men in Jerusalem did after Peter's great sermon on the day of Pentecost, "What shall we do?"[4]

There is a certain logic to a strategy of judgment. After all, the rebellious world *is* under the judgment of God, and the world does need to repent before it is too late. But as with accommodation, the book of Revelation shows us that a strategy of proclaiming judgment more forcefully will not work, because judgment alone will not provoke the rebellious world to repentance.

As John's vision unfolds, the judgment unleashed upon the earth becomes more and more severe. In Revelation 9, terrifying plagues are released on the earth: "By these three plagues a third of mankind was killed, by the fire and smoke and sulfur coming out of their mouths. For the power of the horses is in their mouths and in their tails, for their tails are like serpents with heads, and by means of them they wound" (Rev. 9:18–19 ESV).

And yet look at how the chapter closes: "The rest of mankind, who were not killed by these plagues, did not repent of the works of their hands nor give up worshiping demons and idols of gold and silver and bronze and stone and wood, which cannot see or hear or walk, nor did they repent of their murders or their sorceries or their sexual immorality or their thefts" (vv. 20–21 ESV).

Despite their suffering under the judgment of God, the people do not repent! The plagues mentioned here in Revelation remind us of the plagues the Lord visited upon Pharaoh and the Egyptians, and just as with Pharaoh, the people here do not turn back from sin even after seeing God's judgment firsthand. This is both terrifying and yet obviously true: Judgments alone do not lead people to repent. Look at the dire rates of recidivism among ex-offenders—despite already being convicted and imprisoned for crime, many felons go right back into the same activities and lifestyles that caused them to lose their freedom in the first place. If prison won't cause you to repent, what will? If plagues sent from God won't cause the rebellious world to turn to Jesus, what, then, leads people to repent? Later in John's vision, God sends a violent hailstorm as a sign of judgment on the world, and not only do the people not repent, they curse God rather than change their ways: "From the sky huge hailstones, each weighing about a hundred pounds, fell on people. And they cursed God on account of the plague of hail, because the plague was so terrible" (Rev. 16:21). If we want to reach the world for Christ, we need another strategy than simply proclaiming judgment.

Judgment alone is a dead end, no matter how loudly we shout it.

DEAD END 3: WITHDRAWAL

The church's third option falls between accommodation and judgment—withdrawal. With withdrawal, we do not compromise our beliefs—or at least most of them. We hold to our identity as followers of Christ, but we decide it's just not worth the risk of reaching a lost world. So we give up on reaching the world at all—at least in the short term—and withdraw from the world. In contrast to accommodation, withdrawal means we continue to hold tightly to the truth, but in a defensive posture. We maintain our commitment to Christ—we just withdraw to protect that commitment. Think of it as spiritual hibernation or strategic retreat—we hunker down and hope Jesus returns soon. More than the previous two options, a strategy of withdrawal has much to offer and is worth careful consideration.

One benefit of withdrawal is it preserves the church's distinctiveness. The only way for the church to influence and change a culture is if the church is somehow distinct from it. As Jesus warns us, we need to be salty salt. If the church loses what makes it distinctive—if it loses its saltiness—then it is good for nothing but to be trampled underfoot. Withdrawal from the world removes the temptation to compromise our values and thus saves us from the dead end of accommodation. By withdrawing, we can reemphasize the disciplines that inculcate strong, faithful character in our people. By retreating and raising the drawbridge behind us, we protect ourselves from the danger of accommodation, stubbornly holding on to what makes us different.

There are seasons when withdrawal is necessary. As the British army did when it evacuated from Dunkirk in 1940, the church may need to temporarily beat a strategic retreat so as to survive, regroup, and fight on a future day. There is nothing inherently wrong with the church deciding to isolate itself from the world so it can tend and nurture the things the world needs but does not have. The Amish in America have been doing this for centuries.

Mont-Saint-Michel

Volker Loche/stock.adobe.com

Mont-Saint-Michel, the famous French monastery built on a tidal island in the English Channel, seems like a perfect metaphor for a withdrawn church. Though surrounded by a dangerous flood, a church that is withdrawn from the world will survive by being deliberate in its formative practices, disciplines, and liturgies. It will be isolated but secure.

By withdrawing from the world, the modern church can avoid the fate of the accommodationist churches in Revelation. Rather than give in, we separate ourselves so we can hold even more tightly to the truth. After all, the pressure to compromise with the world is greatest when you are *in* the world. Withdrawal provides some breathing room and lessens the pressure. We raise the drawbridge and flood the moat and, in isolation, make sure that our children are taught to know and love the truth. Withdrawal helps us better focus on Jesus. Perhaps we can be better disciples if we are able to give him more attention, and withdrawal makes that possible.

Yet another positive aspect of withdrawal is that it makes us less likely to draw the attention of the world. One reason a church compromises its beliefs is to avoid the pain of persecution. We might hope to avoid persecution by withdrawing, flying under the radar. Perhaps we will be forgotten—out of sight, out of mind.

But though withdrawal has distinct advantages,* a complete withdrawal is not a viable way forward for the church for a simple reason: It ultimately will not work. We might withdraw for a time, but the world will never ignore the church, no matter how high we build our walls or how

---

* Rod Dreher's 2017 book *The Benedict Option* is precisely about the advantages to the church of a strategic withdrawal. Unfortunately, many commentators missed the point of Dreher's advice, which was for the church to focus on the formation of so-called thick communities in which Christians could practice the spiritual disciplines. In this way, the church would stay "salty" in a post-Christian culture. Although I have a different focus in this book from his in *The Benedict Option*, and though a complete withdrawal cannot be the way forward for the church for the reasons I have set out in this chapter, I do not think my critique really applies to what Dreher calls the Benedict Option—he is correct in suggesting that the church would be well-served by a recovery and emphasis of its ancient spiritual disciplines.

deep we dig our moats. Our existence will soon be viewed as a threat to the dominant secular order, and sooner or later we will be forced to submit at gunpoint. Like the Jews at Masada, we may be able to make a heroic final stand, but in the end we'll be destroyed. The story of Masada is a grim story, but it contains an important truth for the church: The powers that be are not going to be satisfied if we simply withdraw and hide. The church's very existence is a threat to any power that seeks to assert its totalizing authority over and against that of Jesus Christ. Because the church recognizes only Jesus as the rightful lord of the world, as long as the church remains, it is a thorn in the side of any other power that proclaims itself lord. In some ways, the weaker and more isolated the church might seem, the more infuriating it will be to any power that pretends to be ultimate. Bullies particularly hate victims who refuse to cry. Withdrawal as a strategy of survival will lead to persecution, because sooner or later those in power will come for the church anyway.

At this point, some might argue that we *should* withdraw nevertheless and wait for the powers to seek us out. But there is another problem, a theological and missional problem, with a strategy of withdrawal: It is incompatible with the logic of the gospel. Jesus' command in the Great Commission requires us to share the Good News. We cannot claim to be faithful to the gospel and refuse to engage the world. If we withdraw for the sake of faithfulness, we will eventually undermine the faith we are trying to preserve. Like a shark, the church has to move or die.

THE RED THREAD THAT RUNS
BETWEEN ACCOMMODATION,
JUDGMENT, AND WITHDRAWAL

We have seen that in the book of Revelation Jesus warns his church against accommodation and that faithfulness to him requires that they hold on, no matter what; as he puts it to the church in Thyatira, "Hold on to what you have until I come" (Rev. 2:25). And we have seen that judgment alone is not a winning strategy for the church as it seeks to reach the world, because judgment alone is not effective in getting people to repent. But as John walks us through his remarkable vision, we see a larger reason why accommodation, judgment, and withdrawal are dead ends for the church.

Revelation is not just about the end, it is also about the church's role in history as God works all things together for good and history comes to a culmination. What is revelatory about Revelation is that it shows us that the church has a crucial role to play in God's plan to save the world and bring in the kingdom, a role that is explained more clearly in the last book of the Bible than anywhere else in all of Scripture. That role is introduced in Revelation 11, which is the turning point of the entire vision.

Until chapter 11, after the initial warnings to the church against accommodating the false powers of the world, John's vision is mainly concerned with showing the terrifying judgments that the rebellious and wicked world receives as it continues in its evil, unrepentant way. As we have seen, despite the pain it is experiencing, the world would rather curse God than repent. After all the visions of hard-hearted, sinful people, it is therefore somewhat surprising when John does actually see repentance taking place in the rebellious world. The repentance John sees is not brought about through judgment alone, however, but is provoked by the faithful witness of the church to the love of Jesus. In Revelation 11 we read the account of the two witnesses, representing the church in its prophetic ministry to the world, who are martyred for the world. An in-depth commentary on this passage is beyond the scope of this book, but the general sense of what's happening is readily apparent:

"And I will appoint my two witnesses, and they will prophesy for 1,260 days, clothed in sackcloth." They are "the two olive trees" and the two lampstands, and "they stand before the Lord of the earth." If anyone tries to harm them, fire comes from their mouths and devours their enemies. This is how anyone who wants to harm them must die. They have power to shut up the heavens so that it will not rain during the time they are prophesying; and they have power to turn the waters into blood and to strike the earth with every kind of plague as often as they want.

Now when they have finished their testimony, the beast that comes up from the Abyss will attack them, and overpower and kill them. Their bodies will lie in the public square of the great city—which is figuratively called Sodom and Egypt—where also their Lord was crucified. For three and a half days some from every people, tribe, language and nation will gaze on their bodies and refuse them burial. The inhabitants of the earth will gloat over them and will celebrate by sending each other gifts, because these two prophets had tormented those who live on the earth.

—REVELATION 11:3–10

In the vision, the church ("the two witnesses") calls the world to repentance ("sackcloth" is the clothing of the repentant), but though the church is protected for its ministry, nevertheless the enemy opposes it and kills its members. The dead servants of God lie in the streets of "Sodom and Egypt— where also their Lord was crucified"—that is, wherever the church is persecuted (v. 8). And then the wicked people of the earth have a demonic version of Christmas, exchanging gifts and celebrating the violence done to the church: "The inhabitants of the earth will gloat over them and will celebrate by sending each other gifts" (v. 10). It is the same picture we've seen previously—the world refusing to repent.

But then something amazing happens—God vindicates his servants' testimony and proves he has not abandoned them: "But after the three and a half days the breath of life from God entered them, and they stood on their feet, and terror struck those who saw them. Then they heard a loud voice from heaven saying to them, 'Come up here.' And they went up to heaven in a cloud, while their enemies looked on" (vv. 11–12). God has not abandoned his martyrs,[5] and the watching world sees his love for his people.

Up to this point, nothing has yet to break through the hard

63

hearts of the rebellious world. But now, as a result of the signs of judgment around them and the testimony and vindication of God's witnesses, John sees that "the survivors were terrified and gave glory to the God of heaven" (v. 13)! It is a remarkable, moving scene—the first time in the vision that people have turned back to God. And what has provoked it? The testimony and martyrdom of the witnesses—the church. The rest of John's vision explains how the church can fully participate in God's plan to save the world and shows the threats the church will face. Then the vision ends with the return of Jesus and the renewal of all things.

What Revelation reveals to us is that the church's entire purpose is to *go* into a rebellious world and tell it about the love of God.

THE ONLY TRUE OPTION: GO

In light of our culture's increasing hostility to the gospel, what do we do now? How should we engage? We could accommodate, letting go of the gospel and making peace with the world, but Jesus has clearly spoken to his church about the danger of accommodation. "Because you are lukewarm—neither hot nor cold—I am about to spit you out of my mouth" (Rev. 3:16). An accommodationist church has no future with Jesus. Accommodation is not an option.

We could choose judgment, shouting more loudly and preaching judgment more stridently. But again, Revelation reveals that judgment alone does not lead to repentance. This shouldn't surprise us, because judgments never produced repentance in the Old Testament, either—the Exodus story of Pharaoh and the plagues are a particularly good example of the limits of the use of judgment to lead to repentance. The reason that judgment alone cannot be the way forward for the church is because judgment alone does not tell the world about God's mercy. If God wanted to bring a final cataclysmic judgment on the world, he already would have. The reason he patiently forbears to bring a full and final judgment on his rebellious creation is because he is giving people time to repent. As Peter tells us, "The Lord is not slow in keeping his promise, as some understand slowness. Instead he is patient with you, not wanting anyone to perish, but everyone to come to repentance" (2 Peter 3:9). How will the world know the mercy of God if all we proclaim is the coming judgment? Judgment alone is a dead end.

We could choose withdrawal. But withdrawal is the other side of the same coin—judgment on one side, withdrawal on the other. The world on its own cannot know the Good News. The world does not know the love of God, his offer of mercy, and his eagerness to save sinners. Neither loud proclamations of judgment nor a strategy of withdrawal will make the Good News known. While the message of judgment is true— the world needs to repent before it is too late!—without the church's faithful proclamation of the gospel, the rebellious world will never know that Jesus died to save sinners. It is the church's faithful witness to the gospel in the face of a hostile world that is God's plan to fulfill the Great Commission. In Revelation, it is the testimony of the two witnesses that leads the world to repent. And this is why withdrawal, though it can be beneficial for a season, is not a viable long-term option for the church. The Amish have held on to the faith and resisted accommodation to the world, but they have had limited influence in American society and have not been at the forefront of reaching the world for Christ. Both a strategy of judgment and a strategy of withdrawal end up with the same problem: Such strategies make it impossible for the church to actually share the good news of God's love to a rebellious and sinful world.

If we withdraw from the world, we then fail to take our rightful place in God's sovereign plan for history—the place God offers us as his messengers who proclaim the good news of Jesus. This is how Paul puts it in his letter to the Romans: "How then will they call on him in whom they have not believed? And how are they to believe in him of whom they have never heard? And how are they to hear without someone preaching? And how are they to preach unless they are sent? As it is written, 'How beautiful are the feet of those who preach the good news!'" (Rom. 10:14–15 ESV). A church that withdraws is not a witness to the world. Withdrawal is contrary to our stated mission. And if the church rejects its mission, then it is no longer the church. Withdrawal as a strategy to preserve the church will ultimately destroy the church because what makes the church the church is its obedience to Jesus, and Jesus has told us to go. Withdrawal is a dead end.

Not accommodation. Not judgment. Not withdrawal. No,

the only faithful option before the church is to go. This fourth option assumes that Jesus' command to go and make disciples from every people group on earth is still binding and that his Spirit is still guiding us onward. If we truly love God, we will be obedient to his clear command, and if we truly love our neighbors, we will want them to know the truth that will set them free. If we really believe the gospel—that God has love and mercy for everyone, even his enemies—then we must resolve to walk through fire to tell people that Good News. Although the task before us is without precedent—to evangelize a post-Christian culture—the broad mission of the church is still the same as it has been for two thousand years: Go and make disciples.

Going forward to evangelize the world is our only real option. Jesus has given his church the privilege and responsibility of bearing witness to the love of God in a world that doesn't know that love. Without the witness of the church, the world will never know that "God so loved the world that he gave his one and only Son, that whoever believes in him shall not perish but have eternal life. For God did not send his Son into the world to condemn the world, but to save the world through him" (John 3:16–17). Unless the church goes to the world and proclaims the Good News, the world will never repent. This is what Jesus means when he speaks of a city on a hill and a light on a lampstand: "You are the light of the world. A city set on a hill cannot be hidden. Nor do people light a lamp and put it under a basket, but on a stand, and it gives light to all in the house. In the same way, let your light shine before others, so that they may see your good works and give glory to your

Father who is in heaven" (Matt. 5:14–16 ESV). The church has a special message for the world, and when the church refuses to share that message, it no longer has any purpose—a church that isn't sharing the Good News is as nonsensical as a lamp under a bushel basket. The implication is clear: The church needs to go.

Accommodation would mean a church without distinctiveness, judgment would mean a church without success, withdrawal would mean a church without purpose. What do we do now? Our only option is to move forward. To use a phrase I will explain in greater detail later, our best and indeed only option is to go *first*.

But before we get there, there is a peculiar characteristic of the modern world we must take into account as we form a strategy for success—our culture's preference for feelings over facts. If we want to overcome divisions and reach the people who hate us, well-reasoned arguments will not be enough.

DISCUSSION QUESTIONS

1. We have looked at how the West was shaped by the church. What would life in the West look like if another religion became the dominant cultural force going forward?
2. Of the three dead-end options in front of the church, which do you find most tempting? Least tempting?
3. What about Daniel enabled him to choose faithfulness when it mattered? How does one form character like that?

4. If a faithful church is salt to a society, who loses when the church loses its saltiness? Can you think of examples from history?

5. Why does judgment alone not provoke people to repentance? Why didn't Pharaoh repent?

6. What would a withdrawn church lose because of its absence from the world? Is it possible to develop spiritual strength without facing opposition?

WHY FEELINGS DON'T CARE ABOUT YOUR FACTS

In the negative world, it is tempting for the church to congratulate itself on just speaking the truth, shouting the facts. But we live in a time when, more than ever, people prioritize feelings over facts. This is how we got here.

Jesus answered, "You say that I am a king. In fact, the reason I was born and came into the world is to testify to the truth. Everyone on the side of truth listens to me." "What is truth?" retorted Pilate.

—JOHN 18:37–38

Jonathan Haidt is a professor at New York University who has made a career of studying why people believe what they believe. His 2006 book, *The Happiness Hypothesis*, contains a pithy illustration of the difference between facts and feelings, one I have found helpful in understanding modern American culture.[1]

We often seek to persuade other people by giving them the facts: "Here are the seven reasons why you are wrong." We do so because we believe that if people just heard the facts, they would change. But this fact-first approach assumes that people are primarily rational. The problem, says Professor Haidt, is that people are not primarily rational but emotional.

Imagine a rider and an elephant. Haidt makes the case that a person's reason and emotions relate to each other much the way a rider relates to an elephant. The rider can give direction, but if the elephant doesn't want to go that way, then all the impassioned arguments the rider can muster won't change the elephant's course. According to Haidt, our reason is like the rider and our emotions are like the elephant—and elephants are powerful.

Little children are often completely under the control of their emotions. Toddlers throw tantrums over the dumbest things! Every parent quickly learns that trying to calmly reason with a toddler is like trying to reason with an elephant. But, fortunately, humans are meant to grow up, and one of the things grown-ups learn how to do is gain control over their emotions. In the same way, despite an elephant's power, an experienced rider working with a trained elephant actually can influence which direction the elephant chooses to go. But you have to know what you're doing.

It is possible for us to reach the people that hate us and overcome division, but if we rely on facts alone to make our case, we will fail. As we've already seen, Scripture teaches us that judgment alone will not provoke people to repentance. Nevertheless, shouting the facts more stridently can be an alluring temptation for the church—after all, if just we speak the facts often enough and loudly enough, people will eventually understand and agree with us, right? We are like the stereotypical American abroad who thinks that if he just speaks English a bit LOUDER AND SLOWER, the French-speaking waiter will understand.

None of this is to say that facts are irrelevant. I can imagine someone saying, "The gospel is true no matter if the world accepts it; sinners need to repent, whether or not they want to hear about repentance; Jesus is risen whether or not the world believes in him." I agree. The gospel is still true. Sinners need to repent. The empty tomb is a stone-cold fact. Yes, the facts matter. But what happens when people won't listen to the facts?

FACTS AND FEELINGS

"Facts don't care about your feelings" is one of the oft-repeated catchphrases of conservative commentator and media personality Ben Shapiro.[2] On the one hand, I agree with what Shapiro means when he uses that glib phrase: that just because we wish something were true doesn't make it so. Reality has a way of punching back at you, and objective reality isn't changed by your subjective feelings. You can rage or whine or throw a tantrum when you miss your flight, you can berate the gate agent, you can post an obscene and enraged video on social media, but the fact is still stubbornly staring you in the face that the airplane has already left the ground and you're not on it. One of the signs that you are a grown-up is the ability to accept that facts don't care about your feelings. In a sense, *the* mark of maturity is an acceptance of the cold, hard facts, regardless of how they make you feel. There really is no sense crying over spilled milk; it's much wiser to quit crying and start cleaning.

More than that, it is when we take responsibility to *affect* the facts—to change what is within our power to change—that we become whom God created us to be. In the first chapter of the Bible we learn why humanity was created:

> Then God said, "Let us make mankind in our image, in our likeness, so that they may rule over the fish in the sea and the birds in the sky, over the livestock and all the wild animals, and over all the creatures that move along the ground."

> So God created mankind in his own image,
> in the image of God he created them;
> male and female he created them.

God blessed them and said to them, "Be fruitful and increase in number; fill the earth and subdue it. Rule over the fish in the sea and the birds in the sky and over every living creature that moves on the ground."

—GENESIS 1:26–28

What does it mean to be created in God's image? One of the implications of the startling idea that we are made in our creator's image is that humans are created to be creators—we fulfill our purpose when we take on the responsibility of making something out of what's around us. Or as the writer of Genesis puts it, to be fruitful and multiply. But allowing ourselves to be ruled by our feelings and failing to deal with the reality around us arrests our development and keeps us from engaging the world in which we find ourselves. It is only after we decide that some facts can be changed that bridges get built and cakes get baked and books get written. To push aside our emotions so we can more clearly see the facts, and then to decide to change those facts—that's part of what it means to be fully human. The facts around us won't be changed just because we feel a certain way. Civilization itself depends on people deciding to work to change the facts around them; no one ever built or baked anything through feelings alone. Facts are as unaffected by feelings as Mount Rushmore is by the weather. And speaking of weather, is there a better example of the impotence of feelings to change facts? Not a single whining complaint about the weather ever actually changed it.

The example of the brave young black men who sat at

segregated lunch counters during the Jim Crow era is worth considering. Undoubtedly they hated the Jim Crow laws, laws based on the assumption that people who looked like them were less human than other people. And yet they took those feelings of hatred and resentment and then acted. There were many ways they could have responded. They could have chosen physical violence. They could have allowed their emotions to overwhelm their reason and acted unwisely. But they chose to unite their feelings with a wise assessment of their situation and acted accordingly, and our country changed as a result.

One of the great problems with contemporary higher education is that our young people are being permanently infantilized because we are teaching them to prioritize feelings above facts, a manner of instruction that will ultimately benefit neither them nor us. What college students need to be taught instead is that maturity and power come from learning to control their emotions and not be controlled by them. Otherwise, they will be incapable of actually accomplishing anything that matters, or living lives of contentment and accomplishment. When we teach young people to live in thrall to their emotions, we doom them to lives of unhappy ineffectiveness.

So I agree with Ben Shapiro: Facts don't care about your feelings. It's time to grow up and recognize that. But this is also a fact: People aren't changed by facts alone; they are changed by how they feel. In this light, the statement that "facts don't care about your feelings" betrays a fundamental misunderstanding of what motivates people and makes life meaningful: how we feel about the world and our place in it. Facts are stubborn things, and feelings can be rather slippery, but how we feel often determines how we interpret the facts. When it comes to how we perceive and make decisions in our everyday lives, feelings can be more important than facts. And, though we live in a culture that proudly proclaims to value the facts that science and rationality give us, we are more under the control of feelings than ever. Let me explain how this has happened.

HOW SCIENCE MADE US THINK
WE WERE MAINLY THINKERS

For a few hundred years in the West we have been under the impression that a human being is a rational animal, a wet computer, so to speak. We are under this impression because of the remarkable powers that scientific discoveries have made possible, and because of the many ways we are now able to manipulate the material world according to our desires. As scientific discoveries opened up new possibilities and powers and early scientists successfully discovered and then explained physical laws, philosophers became persuaded that reason alone was enough to govern and guide humanity. A specific picture of the human being emerged from the work of these philosophers, and it was the picture of a person who, when properly educated, was rational and intelligent and had no place for superstitions and feelings, a person who would be guided by facts. But this view of the human being as primarily a thinker is false. Though the ability to reason is an important part of human identity, it is not the only part of that identity—the human is not just a thinker but also a feeler. Human beings feel, and what we feel—what we love and desire—shapes how we think and perceive the world around us. In many ways, what we feel precedes what we think.

Our failure to understand the primacy of feelings over facts is partially why we are where we are in America today—in a place where we readily dismiss facts that don't fit our feelings. Humans have always been feeling creatures, but modern American culture has at times elevated feelings far above facts. This can't and won't continue forever—facts are too stubborn to be ignored indefinitely—and it's not going to end well for us if we don't change. You don't break the law of gravity, the law of gravity breaks you. The good news is that change is possible, but changing our culture requires us to understand how we got here. Once we understand that, we'll have a way forward, if we're willing to take the risk and go for it.

For centuries the technological and scientific knowledge of humanity increased relatively slowly, but about five hundred years ago the pace of increase picked up as new discoveries of how the world works became more frequent, each breakthrough building on the next. This burst of scientific advancement is sometimes referred to as the Scientific Revolution.[3] One of the hallmarks of the Scientific Revolution was the discovery that nature seems to be governed by invisible laws—laws such as gravity, for example. These laws aren't arbitrary and irrational but consistent and discoverable by rational inquiry and experimentation. No matter where you are—even sitting under an apple tree in England, as in the case of Sir Isaac Newton—an apple always falls the same way.

It's hard to overstate the implications of believing the world is ordered and comprehensible if you just work hard enough to understand it. Even if you don't have the picture on the box to go by, if you are convinced that the jumble of puzzle pieces in front of you does make a picture when properly placed together, you'll keep at it until the picture appears. And this is what happened: Over a couple of hundred years, in different parts of the world, men and women of curious, methodical dispositions made discovery after discovery about the laws that govern the world, and each discovery provided more motivation for other people to keep methodically inquiring into the problems that had captured their curiosity and interest. And how did these early scientists make their discoveries? Through rational inquiry. They understood that if the world is rational and ordered, then rational thought is necessary to unlock reality's treasure chest of possibility. Rationality was the key, and the startling developments that came so quickly seemed to prove that nothing made man more powerful than when he used his God-given reason to study the world in which God had placed him.

And so two big developments resulted from the Scientific Revolution. The first is obvious: amazing technological changes and breakthroughs, which continue today. The second is less obvious: a change in how people think because of the emphasis on and importance of reason in scientific inquiry. And so the Scientific Revolution brought more than technological change, it also led to shifts in philosophy. The two-hundred-year period (roughly 1600–1800) after the Scientific Revolution is often called the Enlightenment because the leading thinkers in the West during that period felt as if they were shining the light of reason into the minds of men. Because rational thought had been so valuable in scientific advancement, Enlightenment thinkers understandably privileged rational thought above other forms of human knowledge and wisdom.

Why this shift happened isn't mysterious. As a result of scientists' rational inquiry, humans became more and more knowledgeable about the world and demonstrated this growing knowledge through mechanical innovation. Each innovation and discovery only made people feel more impressed with the power of reason. It seemed obvious that if reason could give humanity such control over the material world, then an emphasis on reason was what was needed to govern human life. Whereas in previous "dark ages" humanity was governed by superstition and divine revelation, in the age of the Enlightenment people would walk toward utopia in the bright light of reason.

The idea of rational thought sweeping away superstition and religion was powerful, and each victory of rationality over religion seemed to further prove its power. This is why the famous story of Galileo arguing with the Roman Catholic Church had such a hold on modern thought—it seemed to perfectly illustrate the power of rational thought over religious closed-mindedness. The church insisted that the earth was the center of the solar system, but Galileo argued—drawing on his research—that the sun was the center, and that the earth revolved around the sun. Galileo was correct, of course, and he now functions as a secular saint for modern Western culture, his life supposedly illustrating the utter stupidity and stubbornness of organized religion, particularly of the Christian variety. (Galileo's actual story is of course much more nuanced than the YouTube version, particularly because Galileo himself was a pious Roman Catholic Christian.) Once again, rationality won out.

In the Bible, God is the center of all things, and man's life revolves around God (and not the other way around.) What modern scientific inquiry proved was that when it comes to our solar system, man moves around the sun. What is ironic, however, is that the modern secular project that started during the Enlightenment has actually put man back at the center of the universe. Not literally, of course. But the result of modern thought has actually been to put the individual—me, I—at the center of all things. In how we think these days, the self is at the center, and the world revolves around it.

This is how it happened.

"I THINK, THEREFORE I AM"

René Descartes was a French philosopher in the seventeenth century who was trying to answer the question, "Of what am I certain?" He wanted to find a foundation apart from divine revelation—a secular starting point apart from Scripture—on which one could stand firm and perceive the world outside of oneself, and he did not want to have to rely on past tradition or other authorities. But if you do not want to rely on divine revelation or traditional sources of authority, where do you begin? As a response to this question, he had a piercing insight: "I think, therefore I am." The place to begin was one's own first-person perspective! Descartes knew his own thought wasn't an illusion or a dream. It was real. This was the starting point, and from here one could begin to explore reality with certainty. You start with the fact that you think and then move outward to study the world.

Historians call this insight the Cartesian Revolution: "Cartesian," because of the name Des*cartes*, and "Revolution," because it made the individual's perspective the starting point of knowledge. In previous cultures, outside authorities were the starting point—what God or the gods or the wise men said—and for a person to be wise he needed to submit himself to those authorities. Descartes started a revolution by inverting that idea, and the unintended consequences of Descartes' revolution have brought us full circle back to Galileo, except the positions are now reversed. Descartes believed that if one started with rational reflection upon one's own conscious thoughts, one could then learn and know things about the world. Now, Descartes was not a relativist who believed that whatever an individual believed was his or her truth. But his philosophical approach did shift the starting point for certainty from outside a person to internal to a person. And the problem was that, over the centuries, his ideas were twisted so that today in popular culture what one feels internally has been elevated above objective reality outside oneself—feelings are everything.[4] In Galileo's time the Roman church insisted that the solar system moved around man, but today it is secular society arguing that man (or more specifically the individual's feelings) are what is most important, while religious faith holds that there is an objective reality that exists apart from us and lies at the center, and we—and our feelings—merely orbit around it. Now because my own perspective is the center—"I" am the only sure foundation on which to establish rational inquiry—I have subtly flipped things around so that the world must conform itself to me and what I believe.

Previous cultures believed that the gods or God created the world and that through divine revelation these gods or God gave mankind insight into the world. In these cultures, meaning was found outside yourself, and the way to live a good life was to live in accordance with these external realities. There was reality, and there was you, and growing up and growing wise meant adapting your beliefs and feelings to fit reality.

Before the modern period, this is how virtually all cultures saw the world: Some things just cannot be changed, so instead you must change yourself. Truth exists outside you, and if you're not willing to change from the inside out, the truth will break you in the same way gravity will break you if you fall from a high place. But Descartes changed all that. Or to be more precise, the consequences of the Cartesian Revolution led us to prioritize ourselves over whatever was outside us. Descartes himself was a learned philosopher and a man who valued rationality and objective truth, but his ideas have steadily dripped down through the centuries, leading us to a cultural moment here in the West where feelings, not rational thought, are at the center.

For many people today in Western culture, what is true is what we feel. This is why people talk about "my truth" or "your truth," meaning something is true because *I* feel that it is true, and what is true is whatever I *feel* is true. When Descartes began with the individual's first-person perspective as the foundation for exploring reality, it was a radical idea—a new starting point for establishing a truth claim. What Descartes began, Steve Jobs finished—the smartphone has caused me to turn even further inward, and the way we use these small computers that we all constantly gaze upon has caused us to believe that we—and specifically our desires—are what matters: The world is at our fingertips, ready to rush to meet our every desire. When you tell people today that reality begins with each of them, they don't need much convincing; this is just the air we breathe nowadays. What's scary is that that air is poison and is slowly suffocating us. According to the biblical account, we were created for relationship with the Creator, and when we worship ourselves rather than the Creator, when we pretend that we, not God, are at the center of life, it makes us miserable. This is why you can have material prosperity like we do in America and still have people dying of despair; having our material needs met is necessary, but not sufficient for life to be worth living: We also need relationship with God. The truth is that the self—"I"—is not god. God is not me.

Descartes' ideas helped enable the great scientific advancements and discoveries that we see everywhere in our modern, technological culture. You would think that a culture of such scientific advancement would produce people of calm rationality and objectivity. The irony is that these very technological advancements have persuaded people to look inward so that it often seems we care more about the feelings we find inside ourselves than the facts that lie outside.

Humans are remarkably egotistical, and we have no problem believing that the world ought to revolve around us. If you tell people that what seems true from their perspective is the beginning point of knowledge, they will come to believe you and naturally conclude that whatever they feel is the truth. At that point, trying to use reason to argue against their feelings is as useful as trying to strike sparks from a bar of soap with your knuckles.

So is Ben Shapiro correct? Yes, facts do not care about your feelings. In the end, it doesn't matter whether I think the bridge is strong enough, all that matters is whether it *is* strong enough. But while Ben is correct, his statement about facts over feelings is likely going to convince only those who are already convinced of this truth. This is because in a culture in which the individual's feelings are paramount, arguing by reference to facts won't do much to persuade or change minds. It doesn't matter how logical or clear you are in communicating with me, in the end my feelings will always be more right to me than your facts will ever be.

" 'WHAT IS TRUTH?' RETORTED PILATE"

Perhaps the ultimate example of this is what happens when Jesus stands before Pontius Pilate early on Good Friday.

Then the Jewish leaders took Jesus from Caiaphas to the palace of the Roman governor. By now it was early morning, and to avoid ceremonial uncleanness they did not enter the palace, because they wanted to be able to eat the Passover. So Pilate came out to them and asked, "What charges are you bringing against this man?"

"If he were not a criminal," they replied, "we would not have handed him over to you."

Pilate said, "Take him yourselves and judge him by your own law."

"But we have no right to execute anyone," they objected. This took place to fulfill what Jesus had said about the kind of death he was going to die.

—JOHN 18:28–32

Jesus' enemies among the Jewish leaders are dead set on having him executed. Jesus is innocent and they have no facts on their side, but they have plenty of feelings of murderous hatred.

Pilate then goes back inside to question Jesus.

Pilate then went back inside the palace, summoned Jesus and asked him, "Are you the king of the Jews?"

"Is that your own idea," Jesus asked, "or did others talk to you about me?"

"Am I a Jew?" Pilate replied. "Your own people and chief priests handed you over to me. What is it you have done?"

Jesus said, "My kingdom is not of this world. If it were,

my servants would fight to prevent my arrest by the Jewish leaders. But now my kingdom is from another place."

"You are a king, then!" said Pilate.

Jesus answered, "You say that I am a king. In fact, the reason I was born and came into the world is to testify to the truth. Everyone on the side of truth listens to me."

"What is truth?" retorted Pilate.

—VERSES 33–38

In the prologue to John's gospel, we encounter the Greek word *logos*, which nearly all English translations render as "word." "In the beginning was the Word" (John 1:1). *Logos* means "word," but it also means "rational, organizing idea" or "message" or "reason." Or—and this is my own gloss on the word *logos* in those opening verses of John's gospel—"the mind behind the universe." So in John 1:14 when we read "The Word became flesh and dwelt among us" (ESV), it's almost as if you could read it as "The mind behind the universe became flesh and dwelt among us." Jesus is truth in human form. So when Pilate stands facing Jesus, he is facing off against truth himself, and yet Pilate is so concerned with his feelings of ambition and greed and fear that while he is talking to the mind behind the universe, he has the gall to imply that truth is merely whatever someone wants it to be: "What is truth?" This disdainful remark, dismissive of any truth other than power, sets up his next statement. Pilate goes back outside and admits to the mob that he knows Jesus is innocent.

With this he went out again to the Jews gathered there and said, "I find no basis for a charge against him. But it is your custom for me to release to you one prisoner at the time of the Passover. Do you want me to release 'the king of the Jews'?"

They shouted back, "No, not him! Give us Barabbas!"

Now Barabbas had taken part in an uprising.

—VERSES 38–40

The crowd, stirred up by the religious leaders, cries for Barabbas, a known murderer,[5] to be released and bays for the blood of Jesus. Pilate knows that Jesus is innocent, but that fact is less important to him than the feelings of the crowd and his own desire and ambition. The facts are clear, but no one cares.

Again, lest anyone doubt, let me say clearly: I believe in facts and I think rational argument is important. This book itself is a rational argument. I believe in facts because I believe in truth, and the ultimate truth is Jesus; when we know that truth, it does something—it sets us free.[6] I also believe in the importance of rational arguments because I believe God created us as rational creatures in his image, and we glorify God and honor our neighbor when we approach our neighbor and make a rational argument. When we make a rational argument to another human being, we are in effect saying, "I believe you are worthy of being talked to in this way." Making a rational argument is a way of elevating and dignifying your audience. It is a beautiful and essential thing to do, a way of loving one's neighbor. When you appeal to another person's reason, you are saying, "I believe in your inherent dignity, and rather than talking down at you, I'm honoring God's image in you by speaking to you in a rational manner." Even when people are unable or unwilling to receive rational arguments, nevertheless we must continue to make them because of what doing so implies about the dignity of our interlocutors. Making rational arguments is one way we push back against the darkness.

And yet rational arguments alone won't win the day. In a culture in which feeling is king, lecturing people to pay attention to facts will get you nowhere. I believe in facts because I believe in the truth, but *because* I care about the truth, I'm not content to shout facts and leave it at that. No, I want to change things, I want to reach people, and I want to be heard. And because my goal is not to speak but to be heard, I know that facts are not enough. It's Jonathan Haidt's elephant with its rider: The elephant is our emotions and its rider is our reason. The rider can give direction, but if the elephant doesn't want to go that way, then all the impassioned arguments the rider can muster won't change the elephant's course. At some point, we have to stop arguing with the rider and start influencing the elephant.

Knowing that facts are not enough is immensely helpful in explaining why people so rarely respond to carefully reasoned arguments. We scream facts at each other, and yet the facts don't seem to make a difference. If Haidt is right—and I believe he is—this indifference to facts shouldn't surprise us, but it means we need to stop dropping truth bombs. We need to change our line of attack.

Our preference for feelings over facts also helps explain why judgment—even cataclysmic, terrible judgment—does not provoke people to repentance. As Revelation makes clear, people under judgment would rather indulge their anger and curse God than turn back, change their ways, and ask God for mercy: "The rest of mankind, who were not killed by these plagues, did not repent of the works of their hands nor give up worshiping demons and idols of gold and silver and bronze and stone and wood, which cannot see or hear or walk, nor did they repent of their murders or their sorceries or their sexual immorality or their thefts" (Rev. 9:20–21 ESV).

Facts matter because facts describe reality. But facts alone are not enough! If we want to change our culture and get people to listen to our facts, we will need to appeal to their feelings, too.

This is because we're all Othello now.

SHAKESPEARE AND SOCIAL MEDIA: WHY WE ARE ALL OTHELLO NOW

Everywhere you look these days, you see examples of other people doing and saying wicked, reprehensible things. Are people worse than they've ever been? I do not believe so. It's hard to be a student of history and think that modern man is crueler or more wicked than his ancestors. Once you know about the massacres of Nanjing or Amritsar or the Middle Passage or the aftermath of Spartacus's rebellion, you know that people aren't worse today than in previous centuries, they've always been bad. Christians especially should know that things aren't worse now than they've ever been: After all, the central story of our faith is how people killed the incarnate Son of God. It's hard to do much worse than that.

So what is different today? It is the sheer amount and ready availability of information before us that is unique in human history. As a result of this, we are now easily able to see and experience human wickedness. Anytime I pull my phone out of my pocket, I may be confronted with evidence of someone, somewhere, doing or saying something reprehensible. And because outrage captivates eyeballs, and because an entire business model has been built on attracting eyeballs, the algorithms designed by Silicon Valley corporations feed us a constant stream of examples of outrageous things. What really outrages me are examples of People Who Don't Like Me doing or saying outrageous things, and the designers of our programs know this. I am therefore constantly confronted—again, more often than at any other time in human history—with examples of my enemies doing and saying outrageous things. All of this makes it easier for me to hate my enemies more while seeing myself as righteous and good. Each of us is like the Pharisee in the parable saying, "God, I thank you that I am not like other people."[7]

The internet hasn't made people worse, but it is has made it easy for us to see and experience constant reminders of why we don't like the People Who Don't Like Us, while reinforcing that seductive and affirming sense that we are self-righteously superior to them. It should not surprise us, then, that our mistrust of others is so high these days. When people in our tribe say something nasty on social media, we excuse it, because we assume their intentions are good. But when people in the enemy tribe say something nasty, we assume it is both an accurate revelation of their character and a precursor to nasty action. And so we are caught in a vicious cycle: I dislike you, and then you give me a reason to dislike you more; and you're afraid of me, and then I say things that make you feel justified in your fear.

In June 2020 the nonpartisan research group Beyond Conflict released a fascinating report on American polarization based on three surveys taken between November 2018 and November 2019.[8] The surveys asked both Democrats and Republicans to rate members of the other party with regard to the question "How evolved is the other party?" and then to rate how they expected the other side would rate them according to the same question. Democrats gave their views of Republicans and then rated how they thought Republicans would rate them, and vice versa. Consider the results in the diagram.

HOW EVOLVED WE BELIEVE THE OTHER PARTY IS

DEHUMANIZATION DIVIDE

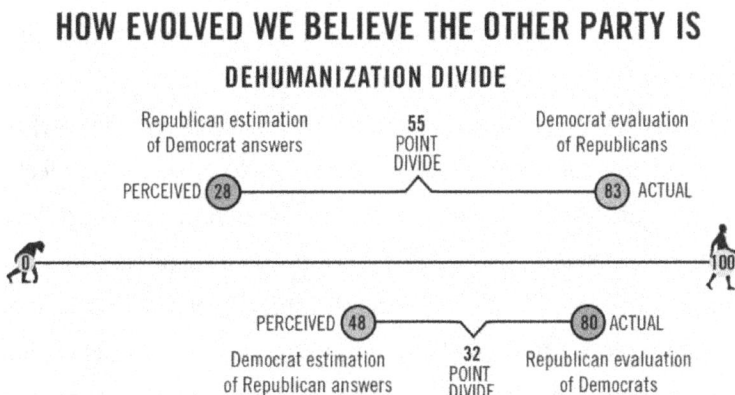

Republican estimation of Democrat answers — 55 POINT DIVIDE — Democrat evaluation of Republicans

PERCEIVED (28) — ⌃ — (83) ACTUAL

0 — 100

PERCEIVED (48) — ⌄ — (80) ACTUAL

Democrat estimation of Republican answers — 32 POINT DIVIDE — Republican evaluation of Democrats

As you can see, there is a wide divergence between what Republicans and Democrats think the other side thinks of them and what the other side actually thinks about them. The thirty-two-point divide between what Democrats think Republicans would say about them and what Republicans actually say about them is bad enough, but the fifty-five-point divide between what Republicans think Democrats would say about them and what Democrats actually say about them should make your blood run cold. Why the difference between the Democrats' and the Republicans' answers? I think it's because the corporate media, Hollywood, and academia are all generally Left-leaning, and so people on the Right have at times in recent years felt more encircled by these cultural institutions than folks on the Left. In any case, you don't have to know very much about history to know that when one group of people thinks that another group despises them, violence could be the result. "Desperate times call for desperate measures" and "It's kill or be killed" are self-fulfilling ideas. Why else would Othello have ever murdered Desdemona?

William Shakespeare's play *The Tragedy of Othello, the Moor of Venice* was written around 1603. The play tells the story of what happens when we allow our thoughts to overwhelm our reality, and when we allow ourselves to be guided by feelings regardless of the facts. In Renaissance Venice, Othello is a general who has a jealous and disappointed lieutenant named Iago. Iago hates Othello for passing him over for promotion and puts in motion an elaborate plot to convince Othello that Desdemona, Othello's new and beloved wife, despises him and is having an affair with one of Othello's subordinates. The story is a lie concocted by Iago, but the lie is just believable enough to put a worm of suspicion in Othello's mind. As the play goes on, Othello becomes more and more convinced of Desdemona's unfaithfulness until he murders her in a fit of rage. As she lies dying, the truth comes out that it was Iago who orchestrated the whole situation. Othello then kills himself in his grief and guilt.

Shakespeare was a literary genius with great insight into human nature, and he knew that it is what we think other people think about us that determines how we act toward them. Every one of us likes people who like us and dislikes people who dislike us. And it's easy to see why this cycle is self-perpetuating. If I think you dislike me, then I'll dislike you, thereby giving you more reason to dislike me, and on and on. How can this dark cycle be broken?

The cycle is broken when someone decides to act rather than react, when one person decides to take the risk and reach out first. As we shall see, this is actually what love looks like— not sentimental feeling but deliberate action.

If Othello had moved toward Desdemona rather than away from her, the tragedy could have been avoided. Instead of choosing to act, however, he allowed himself to react with fear, and his emotions blinded him to the truth until it was too late. In the end, it is irrelevant whether other people are actually a threat to us; what matters is whether we think they are a threat to us. Or to put it another way, our emotions determine how we perceive reality, and it is our perceptions that drive our actions. If I'm a Republican who thinks my Democrat neighbor considers me to be more of an animal than a man, then that thought will shape my perceived reality even though my Democrat neighbor thinks no such thing. In this case, perception really is reality.

Yes, facts matter, because facts describe reality, and reality has a way of painfully reminding us it is there. Yet we also need to recognize that feelings don't care about facts. If we want to win a hearing for the facts, we need to start with changing how people feel. And when it comes to feelings, my mom was right: Other people are more scared of you than you are of them.

DISCUSSION QUESTIONS

1. Describe a time when you could not persuade someone with the facts.
2. How does allowing yourself to be ruled by feelings and emotions hold you back?
3. Do facts matter?
4. Since we were created for relationship with God, how does imagining and living as if we ourselves are the center of everything make us miserable?
5. When Pilate says "What is truth?" he is effectively shutting down the conversation. What are some other ways that people will shut down the conversation when they don't like where the facts are taking them?
6. How has your media consumption affected your emotions?
7. How does making a rational argument dignify one's audience?

OTHER PEOPLE ARE MORE SCARED OF YOU THAN YOU ARE OF THEM

Feelings often trump facts. This would be a depressing
truth if there were no way to influence feelings.
The good news is that there is, and all it takes is
understanding something basic about human nature.

**When a Samaritan woman came
to draw water, Jesus said to her,
"Will you give me a drink?" (His
disciples had gone into the town to
buy food.) The Samaritan woman
said to him, "You are a Jew and I am
a Samaritan woman. How can you
ask me for a drink?" (For Jews do
not associate with Samaritans.)**

—JOHN 4:7–9

When I was a little boy, I lived with my family on the side of a small green mountain in West Africa. Our house on the verdant mountainside was surrounded by mango trees. Mangoes are good for eating and mango trees are good for climbing, and the best mango tree for climbing was the big one at our neighbor's house. Our neighbor lived across a small, shallow valley from our house, and there were two ways to get there: the long way and the short way. The long way was the road, which curved around the side of the valley in a broad loop. Since boys don't like taking the long way, we never took the road. It was far better and faster to cut across the valley, following a small dirt footpath that ran directly to our neighbor's house. This path cut through a shallow bowl of tall reeds and grasses, reeds so tall that once you entered the path, you could see neither right nor left. At times, as my brother and I ran along the path, we'd spot a black form with a red belly rustling and slithering across the path in front of us: a spitting cobra. My love for climbing the good climbing tree at my neighbor's house made me want to cross the valley, but I always did so with a fear of meeting a cobra. I would run along the path so fast it felt as if my feet barely touched the ground.

Our green little mountain was infested with spitting cobras, which are exactly what they sound like: cobras that rear up and spit venom at the eyes of their prey. Once, my nearsighted dad came around the corner of our house and startled one of these snakes, which swayed up and spit venom at him. Fortunately, my nearsighted dad wears glasses, and when he came sprinting back inside the house, we could see the milky venom dripping off his lenses. I've never liked cobras.

My brother and I would whine about the snakes living around us, but my mom adopted her Pollyanna persona and wouldn't accept our complaints. She would tell us, "Boys, they are more scared of you than you are of them." I think she got her herpetological information from that scene in *The Parent Trap* where the gold-digging fiancée is set up by the twins and convinced to tap sticks together to scare off California bears. My mom's advice was essentially to make lots of noise whenever we ran around outside, certain that our noisemaking would scare away any lurking cobras. Sometimes, as we ran across the valley to that wonderful mango tree for climbing, we'd clap our hands and yell like little idiots, hoping that our mom was right and all the cobras were fleeing before us.

But if I'm honest, even as a small boy I had my doubts about the truth of her claim about the psychological state of our neighborhood cobras—"Boys, they're more scared of you than you are of them"—primarily because it didn't seem possible for a venomous, coldhearted reptile to experience terror greater than the kind I felt as an imaginative little boy. Even to this day I do not care for snakes and find it entirely appropriate that the Bible tells us it was a serpent that brought evil into Eden. But now, as an adult, I have decided that my mother was more right than she realized. She may not have known anything about snakes, but her insight is accurate when applied to other people: They tend to be more scared of you than you are of them.

Now, of course, it is not actually true that everyone nearby is walking around in fear of your presence—to say that other people are "more scared of you than you are of them" is a bit tongue-in-cheek. What I mean when I use that phrase is that people are naturally reactive; we observe what others do and how others act before we decide how we will act. To act first, therefore, without regard to how someone else is acting is a radical departure from the natural human tendency. So though other people are probably not shaking in their boots when they see you coming, they are nevertheless naturally inclined to base their actions off whatever you do.

As we've seen, for the first time in history the church is tasked with evangelizing a post-Christian culture. We live in the negative world, where people see Christianity not as something good or even neutral but as something harmful, something to hate and oppose. So how do we proceed? How do we reach the people that hate us? Accommodation, judgment, and withdrawal—none of these are the right answers. The way forward is to go forward. And though it seems counterintuitive and even crazy to move directly toward the people who hate us, the reason it works is because, in a world in which everyone is waiting to react to everyone else, the one who chooses to go first and act will fundamentally change the status quo and thereby open up new possibilities to walk into.

THE FIGHTER PILOT WHO
PLAYED PING-PONG

Imagine two fighter jets engaged in an aerial dogfight. Each pilot tries to outmaneuver the other and achieve positional superiority by placing the enemy within his line of fire. So the airplanes loop and veer and climb and dive, each trying to get behind the other while avoiding falling for the other's feints and tricks. Each pilot has to take into account the physical laws of flight (even the most sophisticated modern jets still obey the laws of physics), the location of the floor (hitting the water or running into a mountain will have the same result as that of being shot down by the enemy—death!), the movements of the enemy (while you are moving at a tremendous rate of speed, so he is), and, crucially, how all of these and many other details affect one another as they are in constant flux. Obviously, the capabilities of the respective aircrafts play a part in a pilot's dogfighting success—a pilot flying a modern airplane would have an advantage over an opponent flying a biplane from World War I. But, as air force pilot John Boyd came to realize, the most important characteristic that victorious fighter pilots shared was not technical superiority but the speed at which they made accurate decisions.

Colonel Boyd has become a cult figure in the modern air force, which is ironic because when he died in 1997, he was, to quote author Robert Coram, "one of the most important unknown men of his time."[1] Not only do American military pilots read his biography and study his tactical principles in pilot training, but his insights into war-fighting strategy have been adopted by the very Department of Defense that shunned him in his later years. Boyd's influence is everywhere.

Boyd's influential insights derived from his personal experience as a fighter pilot. What he realized was that the best way for a pilot to win an aerial dogfight was to make decisions and act more quickly than his opponent. If you can initiate the right action before the other person does, each successive move puts you farther and farther ahead and the other person farther and farther behind. Each action changes the situation and alters the dynamic between you. Boyd developed an acronym that summed up the entire process: the OODA (pronounced "oo-duh") loop.

- Observe
- Orient
- Decide
- Act

The process is a loop because reality is fluid and not static, with new decisions and actions and observations constantly happening, and, with each new datapoint, a new reality being created. The quicker a person can process and then act and then evaluate those actions and then take new actions as a result of that evaluation, the more effective he will be.

Imagine again two fighter pilots in a dogfight. If one pilot can get inside the other's OODA loop, so to speak, he will have the upper hand. The other pilot will try to anticipate and respond to everything the first pilot will do, but, like a wasp struggling in a spider's web, every movement will serve only to further entrap him.[2] To survive he must break the cycle and stop merely reacting to his enemy's move—he must break out and regain the initiative. Say a fighter pilot finds himself in his enemy's crosshairs. If he quickly takes evasive action and is able to loop behind his enemy, he now has the upper hand and has constrained his enemy's choices.

For me, thinking about two players playing a game of ping-pong has been helpful in visualizing Boyd's OODA loop. One player serves, another player returns serve. If the first player is particularly skilled, she can serve the ball in the exact location that will be most difficult for her opponent to return. Let's imagine that player 2 does somehow manage to return the serve, but barely, and then player 1 hits the ball back to the opposite side of the table from where player 2 is standing. Player 2 lunges over, hits the ball back, and then player 1 returns the ball to the other side again. And so on. If player 1 is much more skilled than player 2, each shot she makes only puts her opponent farther and farther behind, until a mistake is made and the point is won. This is an example of the OODA loop in action—player 1 has gotten inside the OODA loop of player 2, and because she was able to more quickly and more effectively make decisions and take actions, she has won the point.

But let us suppose that player 2 is also a skilled ping-pong player. Say player 1 delivers a wicked serve, one that stretches player 2. Let's say the rally lasts for a few returns, one player hitting the ball back over the net, the other player returning, and so on. But let's say, slowly but surely, player 2's superior play has enabled her to get the upper hand so that she finally returns the ball in a way that is unplayable to player 1, and the point is lost. In that case, player 2 was able to outmaneuver player 1 and break out of the OODA-loop trap in which she found herself. The hunted had become the hunter.

The simple takeaway from the OODA loop is that you change a relationship between two parties by being the first one to move. Every choice and action that follows that initial move is merely a response—the first move has permanently altered the relationship between the parties. There is great power in acting while others are simply reacting, whether at the individual or at the organizational level. Anyone who is willing to take a risk and act can bring change to their surroundings. And as Boyd understood, anyone who is wise enough or skilled enough to take the right first action, and to follow up that action with more right actions taken more quickly than the opponent can do, will win.

CONFESSION: I LIKE PEOPLE WHO LIKE ME

In a world filled with division, mistrust, and fear, everyone is watching warily to see how everyone else will act. Every day, we make constant evaluations—are you friend or foe? And so here is an obvious but embarrassing truth I need to confess: I like people who like me. When people approach me and smile and seem actually glad to be with me, I have the same reaction every single time: I like them, too. If I am in a hurry in the grocery-store checkout line, thinking only about what else I have to do that day and hoping to complete my transaction as quickly as possible—if, while in that distracted and hurried state, I see the cashier smiling at me and making eye contact while saying, "How are you doing today, sir?" my busy spell is broken. Often at those times I look back at the cashier with gratitude and say, "You know, it has been a good day." I know I'm not the only one like this. All of us are really that simple: We like the people who like us.

Each of us was made for relationship. God made us to look outward to him and to each other. We are made to connect with others, to be approved of and valued by others. There is even research showing that when musicians play music with one another—even if they are not very adept at their instruments—their hearts begin beating in sync together.[3] But the rebellion in the garden of Eden caused suspicion to replace trust in the heart of the human being. And though we desperately need to be loved, we are now also wary of being harmed. We keep our fists up, circling the other person, ready to hit back hard if he or she hits us. We have become at times like junkyard dogs, growling and snarling and circling one another, trying to determine whether the other is a threat. Some people spend their entire lives in that attitude.

But what if we can break through the other person's defenses and change the relationship or reset its course? What if instead of trying to land the first punch, we took off our gloves and walked palms up toward the other person? How would the relationship change?

JESUS AND THE OODA LOOP

Jesus, if I could be permitted to say so, was a master of using the OODA loop to his advantage. In the Gospels, he is constantly getting the upper hand in his personal interactions. If, through the course of an interaction, it is clear that his interlocutors are closed to his message, then Jesus will maneuver them in such a way as to make an important teaching point. Consider, for example, how smoothly he plays it in the famous "render to Caesar what is Caesar's, and to God what is God's" incident, which Mark, in his account of the interaction, concludes with a little flourish: "And they were amazed at him."[4] When the interaction is with an enemy, Jesus always comes out on top. But, with those who are open to the truth, Jesus will maneuver his interlocutors into places where meaningful conversation and revelation can happen.

Jesus' mastery of the interpersonal is clearly seen in his interaction with the Samaritan woman in John 4:4–26. The account begins tamely enough:

> Now he had to go through Samaria. So he came to a town in Samaria called Sychar, near the plot of ground Jacob had given to his son Joseph. Jacob's well was there, and Jesus, tired as he was from the journey, sat down by the well. It was about noon.

It is implied that the spring is a ways out of town, and because the disciples have gone into the town to buy food, Jesus is there alone when a Samaritan woman approaches:

When a Samaritan woman came to draw water, Jesus said to her, "Will you give me a drink?" (His disciples had gone into the town to buy food.)

The Samaritan woman said to him, "You are a Jew and I am a Samaritan woman. How can you ask me for a drink?" (For Jews do not associate with Samaritans.)

Jesus begins innocuously enough—"Can I have some water?"—but there is a sly strategy behind the question, as the woman's shocked response shows. In the time of Jesus, Jews considered Samaritans to be half-breeds, Israelites who had intermarried with gentiles centuries before. Samaritans were considered unclean, and they were viewed as heretics, not true believers. They read the Torah (the first five books of the Old Testament) but rejected everything else in the Hebrew Bible: the Psalms, the Prophets, and many other books. Instead of in Jerusalem, they believed the Lord should be worshiped on Mount Gerizim. The Jews knew the Samaritans were wrong, and in some ways more dangerously wrong than if they had been ignorant pagans, because the Samaritans had part of the truth, but they had perverted it, which led them into error. In the famous parable of the good Samaritan,[5] the reason Jesus chooses a Samaritan to play the hero is because he knows it will shock his Jewish audience. For a Jew to choose to interact with a Samaritan was remarkable. For a Jewish man to interact with a Samaritan woman? What Jesus does is completely unexpected.

As a result of his unexpected opening gambit, the woman

expresses surprise that Jesus would dare to ask her for a drink. Her surprise allows Jesus to reply in such a way as to begin to steer the conversation in the direction he wants it to go:

> Jesus answered her, "If you knew the gift of God and who it is that asks you for a drink, you would have asked him and he would have given you living water."

Note that Jesus, in the way he so often does, speaks cryptically and in such a way that the listener will misunderstand, a misunderstanding that will require further conversation. "Living water" is an idiomatic expression in Greek for "running water." At the spring of Jacob, standing beside the well, Jesus begins to speak of the Holy Spirit,[6] whereas the woman takes his words literally. He says that the life that he brings will be like having a spring of water flowing up out of a person, but she wonders how he will actually draw up running water from the well:

> "Sir," the woman said, "you have nothing to draw with and the well is deep. Where can you get this living water? Are you greater than our father Jacob, who gave us the well and drank from it himself, as did also his sons and his livestock?"

Again, Jesus replies provocatively, drawing the woman out:

> Jesus answered, "Everyone who drinks this water will be thirsty again, but whoever drinks the water I give them will

never thirst. Indeed, the water I give them will become in them a spring of water welling up to eternal life."

The woman said to him, "Sir, give me this water so that I won't get thirsty and have to keep coming here to draw water."

The entire time Jesus has been speaking on one level, and the woman on another. She has been misunderstanding what he is saying, and he is okay with that because his goal is to take the conversation in a more pointed direction. He—again, slyly strategic—asks her to bring her husband so he can speak to him as well:

He told her, "Go, call your husband and come back."

"I have no husband," she replied.

Jesus said to her, "You are right when you say you have no husband. The fact is, you have had five husbands, and the man you now have is not your husband. What you have just said is quite true."

No-fault divorce did not exist in the time of Jesus, and women couldn't initiate divorce in that culture, so it is fair to conclude that this woman has been used and abused by a series of different men. She's a mess. Jesus does not steer the conversation in this personal direction in order to bring up past pain or to pass judgment on her; rather, Jesus is using the discussion about her husbands to signal to her that he is not an ordinary traveler. The move is successful, and he has certainly gotten her attention:

"Sir," the woman said, "I can see that you are a prophet. Our ancestors worshiped on this mountain, but you Jews claim that the place where we must worship is in Jerusalem."

Perhaps the woman wants to talk about theological differences between Jews and Samaritans. Perhaps she just doesn't want to talk about her painful personal situation. Either way, Jesus takes what she says and makes his penultimate move:

"Woman," Jesus replied, "believe me, a time is coming when you will worship the Father neither on this mountain nor in Jerusalem. You Samaritans worship what you do not know; we worship what we do know, for salvation is from the Jews. Yet a time is coming and has now come when the true worshipers will worship the Father in the Spirit and in truth, for they are the kind of worshipers the Father seeks. God is spirit, and his worshipers must worship in the Spirit and in truth."

The Samaritan woman is intrigued by what Jesus is telling her, and she tentatively begins to talk to him about theological issues. Jesus explains to her that God's plan to save the world begins with the Jews, but that once the Spirit comes, the actual place where worship happens will not matter. The temple was the place where God's Spirit "dwelt," but Jesus is now the place where heaven and earth meet,[7] and after his death and resurrection the Holy Spirit will be with all who believe in him.

This discussion of true and proper worship has finally

brought the woman right to where Jesus wants her to be. She shares what she knows about the Jewish Messiah:

> The woman said, "I know that Messiah" (called Christ) "is coming. When he comes, he will explain everything to us."

The moment has arrived. In Samaria (of all places), with a Samaritan woman (of all people), Jesus reveals himself at exactly the right time in exactly the right way:

> Then Jesus declared, "I, the one speaking to you—I am he."

Jesus has been in control throughout the entire interaction. With each question and response and comment, he has brought the woman to the verge of faith and presented her with a decision to either trust him or reject him. (John goes on to show the woman as a model evangelist who brings her entire village to Jesus, so it is clear she has put her faith in him.) The entire interaction is like a perfectly executed dogfight or a perfectly played ping-pong match. Jesus has used the OODA loop to perfection.

While it is significant that Jesus moves first toward the Samaritan woman, transgressing social barriers, what's even more important is that the woman knows that Jesus has reached across a boundary to speak to her. Note her reaction after Jesus' initial words: "You are a Jew and I am a Samaritan woman. How can you ask me for a drink?" She is totally surprised by Jesus' move toward her. This is the power of going first toward another person, particularly when that person is in the wrong—it shocks them into a new frame of mind, one in which they are open to listen and to change.

And it all started with a simple and completely unexpected question: "Can I have some water?"

IT'S TIME TO GO FIRST

What I'm talking about isn't rocket science, though it has explosive power despite its radical simplicity. In a world of increasing polarization and growing mistrust of others, what does the church need to do to overcome that division? Do we let the world set the terms and have the upper hand? Are we planning on always living in response to what others do? Should the church be merely a reactionary community, pushing back against the attacks of the culture in a cultural war? There are moral stands we have to take, no matter what. But I personally am tired of being on the defensive—I'd like to take new ground. The war is not going to be won simply by reacting, and the people who hate us are not going to be reached unless we make the first move. There is a way forward that changes the rules and upends the battle. In light of all that is currently true—a hostile media environment, enraged social-media mobs, the climate of fear in American culture specifically and modern Western culture in general—I believe we need to do more than simply respond. We must go on the offensive. It's time to go first.

THE BALCONY INCIDENT

I once served a church that had a wraparound balcony. One Sunday morning a number of years ago, I was trying to get the attention of our sound guy sitting up in that balcony. But sitting right behind him was another man, someone I knew disliked both me and our church. Whenever he had a chance to complain, he'd let me know what he thought. This man erroneously thought I was waving at him and gave me one of those embarrassed halfhearted waves you give when you realize the other person isn't waving at you at all. We've all been there.

A few hours later I was in the parking lot and saw this man talking with a group of people. As I walked by, I said to him, "I'm sorry about that confusion earlier. I was actually trying to get the sound guy's attention." He somewhat bitterly replied, "That's okay. I just thought you were saying hi to me for once."

I just thought you were saying hi to me for once.

I admit, his response shocked me. Here was a man who had frequently and repeatedly made it no secret that he didn't care for me or my church, who was old enough to be my father, basically telling me he wanted me to like him. *That* guy wants *me* to like *him*? I never would have thought that in a million years. But it was true: He had just admitted as much to me. And since that time, I've come to understand that this is always true. Whether they are aware of it or not, people are constantly waiting to see how you will approach them before they decide how they will respond to you. We are all like fencers circling each other, foils extended—*en garde*—waiting to see how the other will attack. We are like boxers sparring, gloves up, moving around the ring and waiting to see if the other drops his shoulder or telegraphs a punch.

But what happens when you decide to drop your gloves and leave your jaw exposed? What happens when you approach people with both hands extended, palms open, and smile? What happens when you do everything you can to tell them, "I am not a threat"?

The afternoon of the balcony incident, three simple words came into my head, words that immediately made sense to me. If I can be honest with you, I believe those three words were a gift from God, and they are the theme of this book.

LOVE GOES FIRST

Love goes first. Those three words are the message of this book, and we will spend the rest of the book exploring what they mean and examining how to put them into practice. At its heart, that three-word idea is just another way of saying that John Boyd was right, more right than he knew. If you want to change the world, you have to go first.

Now, there is nothing particularly helpful or original in pointing out the obvious fact that it is better to be on the front foot than the back foot. For thousands of years—since the Chinese military theorist Sun Tzu wrote *The Art of War* sometime in the fifth century BC—taking the initiative through surprise or deception or speed has been a basic tenet of military doctrine. But the principle I am proposing in this book is not about going first and taking the initiative for the purpose of selfish gain, power, or control. Going first is not about jumping up as soon as the plane comes to a stop so you can push forward and be the first person off the airplane. Going first as I use the phrase is not about you at all: It's about the other. It's about overcoming division and overturning the status quo. Going first is about being the first one to move toward the other to seek what is best for the other. More than that, as we shall see, going first is the practical way to actually do what Jesus told us to do. Love goes first.

In the negative world, in a world of polarization, how will we reach the people that hate us? Accommodation, judgment, withdrawal—all of these options are dead ends for the church. They will not take us where we need to go. We will not reach the world in those ways. No, the way forward is to take Jesus at his word and go. More specifically, the way forward, the way to overcome division and reach even those who hate us, is to go first. If you want to change the world, you have to go first, because love goes first.

But before we can move forward, we need to be sure we have the right idea about love. It's a word that everyone uses, but, to quote Inigo Montoya, "I do not think it means what you think it means."

DISCUSSION QUESTIONS

1. Can you think of a time when someone showed unexpected or surprising interest or affection toward you? How did that affect you?
2. "Other people are more scared of you than you are of them." Do you agree or disagree with that statement?
3. How might one person making the first move change the status quo between two people?
4. According to the definition provided in this chapter, what does it mean to go first?
5. What is something that Jesus does in his interaction with the woman at the well that makes her receptive to his message?

5

LOVE

"You Keep Using That Word;
I Do Not Think It Means What
You Think It Means"

Many people have the wrong idea of what love is. What do you do when the most important word in the world is the least understood word in the world?

" 'And you shall love the Lord your God with all your heart and with all your soul and with all your mind and with all your strength.' The second is this: 'You shall love your neighbor as yourself.' There is no other commandment greater than these."
—MARK 12:30–31 ESV

The 1987 movie *The Princess Bride* is chock-full of memorable, quotable lines:

- "As you wish."
- "Mawwiage is what bwings us togevuh today."
- "Hello. My name is Inigo Montoya. You killed my father. Prepare to die."

But of all the great lines in the movie, my favorite is delivered by Inigo Montoya after he hears another character repeatedly use the word *inconceivable* to describe situations that are completely conceivable, if just unwanted: "You keep using that word. I do not think it means what you think it means."

When it comes to the word *love*, that's how I feel. As we shall see, there is a vast divide between the world's understanding of love and the Bible's understanding of love. The purpose of this book is to provide a way forward for the church that overcomes division, and if we are going to go in that direction, we have to get clear on just what, exactly, love is.

THE LOVE LAW

In the negative world, in a post-Christian culture, what do we do now? Many Christians will rightly look to the Bible for guidance. The Ten Commandments, for example, are guideposts that tell us what to do, or, more accurately, what not to do.[1] This is one of the reasons the poets of Israel were so grateful for God's word to them—because it gave them insight from God himself on how to live well.

> Oh, how I love your law!
>> I meditate on it all day long.
> Your commands are always with me
>> and make me wiser than my enemies.
>
> —PSALM 119:97–98

This idea, that God's people had insight into life that other peoples did not have, was an important part of Jewish self-understanding. In his letter to the Romans, the apostle Paul spells out the role that God's people could play among the unbelieving nations because they had been specifically chosen to receive God's law.[2] Paul, speaking to an imaginary Jewish interlocutor, explains that a person who knows God's law is "a guide for the blind, a light for those who are in the dark, an instructor of the foolish, a teacher of little children, [all] because you have in the law the embodiment of knowledge and truth" (Rom. 2:19–20).

So one of the ways Israel understood itself to be set apart

from the nations was because of its possession of God's law—the Israelites knew how to live rightly, and they were grateful. And even though Israel was never truly able to follow the law's guidance, the very fact that Israel fell short of the law was a sign of its value as a guide—the law was true north, and Israel's behavior was measured by it.

But though the Ten Commandments and the other laws that Moses received on Mount Sinai provide guardrails for our actions, there are still many situations in which it can be confusing to know exactly what we are supposed to do. One aspect of Jesus' teaching ministry therefore was to speak to the intention behind the law and thereby highlight what God expected of his people so they could live well in his world. Jesus provided this insight into the purpose of the law so that his followers could apply it to their lives. For example, in the Sermon on the Mount, when Jesus taught on the commandment about murder, he explained that God's desire is deeper than for us to simply refrain from murder. Rather, the sixth commandment is also meant to point people toward reconciliation and kindness:

> "You have heard that it was said to the people long ago, 'You shall not murder, and anyone who murders will be subject to judgment.' But I tell you that anyone who is angry with a brother or sister will be subject to judgment. Again, anyone who says to a brother or sister, 'Raca' [a term of contempt], is answerable to the court. And anyone who says, 'You fool!' will be in danger of the fire of hell.

"Therefore, if you are offering your gift at the altar and there remember that your brother or sister has something against you, leave your gift there in front of the altar. First go and be reconciled to them; then come and offer your gift."

—MATTHEW 5:21–24

So if I am wondering what to do when there is bad blood between me and someone else in church, the Lord wants me to pursue reconciliation. That's helpful. But what about other situations in which I find myself and for which there doesn't seem an exact precedent or biblical commandment to apply? People in Jesus' day wondered the same thing.

The Bible teaches that wisdom comes from learning to fear the Lord, and the way we do that is by obeying his commandments. As Psalm 111 puts it, "The fear of the Lord is the beginning of wisdom; / all those who practice it have a good understanding," (Ps. 111:10 ESV). But of the hundreds of commandments, which is most important? If I remember the Sabbath day and cease from work (Ex. 20:8), is it then wrong for me to love my neighbor as myself (Lev. 19:18) and help him pull his ox out of a ditch on the Sabbath?

People in Jesus' day wondered the same thing. The Gospels relate how, approaching Jesus while he was in the temple courts in Jerusalem, one of the religious leaders of the Jews asks Jesus which commandment is the greatest. Although the question is likely meant to trap Jesus, it's still a great question—if you know which is greatest, then when you are in a sticky moral situation, you can know what to do by knowing which command takes precedent. The scribe who puts the question to Jesus is asking Jesus to give some guidance: What is the goal of the Law? Jesus answers him by combining two Old Testament commandments together:

> And one of the scribes came up and heard them disputing with one another, and seeing that he answered them well, asked him, "Which commandment is the most important of all?" Jesus answered, "The most important is, 'Hear, O Israel: The Lord our God, the Lord is one. And you shall love the Lord your God with all your heart and with all your soul and with all your mind and with all your strength.' The second is this: 'You shall love your neighbor as yourself.' There is no other commandment greater than these." And the scribe said to him, "You are right, Teacher. You have truly said that he is one, and there is no other besides him. And to love him with all the heart and with all the understanding and with all the strength, and to love one's neighbor as oneself, is much more than all whole burnt offerings and sacrifices." And when Jesus saw that he answered wisely, he said to him, "You are not far from the kingdom of God." And after that no one dared to ask him any more questions.
>
> —MARK 12:28–34 ESV

And so when Jesus was pressed to rank the commandments and name which was the "greatest commandment," he brilliantly sums up all of the Bible's principles with a simple two-part formula:

1. Love God.
2. Love your neighbor as yourself.[3]

In the same vein, the apostle Paul puts it like this in his letter to the Romans: "The commandments, 'You shall not commit adultery,' 'You shall not murder,' 'You shall not steal,' 'You shall not covet,' and whatever other command there may be, are summed up in this one command: 'Love your neighbor as yourself.' Love does no harm to a neighbor. Therefore love is the fulfillment of the law" (Rom. 13:9–10).

All of the commandments God has provided to his people can be distilled down to one key idea: love. In any and every situation the right thing to do or the action that fulfills God's will or the way to best live is to love. Whenever we struggle to answer the question, What do I do now? the right answer is always the same: love.

WHAT IS LOVE?

That sounds simple. But we immediately run into difficulty, because *love* in English is a confusing word. It has a vast range of meanings, and if I am looking for guidance on what exactly to do, I can still end up lost. What does love look like? Because of our confusion about just what, exactly, love is, it's very easy for this Great Commandment to become nothing more than sentimental mush. Many of us have no clear idea what love is. In fact, I think *love* happens to be one of the least understood words in the world.

Our first problem with love is that, in modern America, our dominant cultural understanding of love is what the ancient Greeks would have described as erotic—the love between men and women, usually with a sexual undertone. Just think of how thoroughly dedicated pop music is to erotic love:

- "All You Need Is Love"
- "I Will Always Love You"
- "You Give Love a Bad Name"

Now consider how many popular movies have been made since the 1960s that have romantic love as a main theme. All of these pop-cultural influences mean that for many people in our culture, their conception of love is along the lines of that expressed in the movie *Sleepless in Seattle*—a man and a woman fall in love and then (we presume) live happily ever after.

But there are two problems with thinking of love as primarily erotic:

1. It is limiting. The vast majority of our relationships are not meant to be in the erotic category. Our relationships with our children, our parents, our siblings, our colleagues—none of these relationships are meant to be erotic. If we add eroticism into these relationships, we ruin them.

2. More important for Christians, the idea of love as being primarily erotic is not found in the Bible. There is some eroticism in the Bible (in addition to the well-known

example of David and Bathsheba, also see the interaction between Potiphar's wife and Joseph, or the definitely-not-for-children story of Samson and Delilah, or the strange story of Esther and her seduction of the Persian king, or just read any verse from the Song of Solomon at random!), but as we shall see, the Bible's primary sense of love has nothing to do with eroticism at all.[4]

If you have ever looked up a word like *love* in a dictionary, you'll have noticed that there are several definitions given. This is because most words—and especially common, simple words—have a semantic range. They are capable of meaning lots of different things, depending on the context in which they are used. Take a common English word such as *talk*, for example. *Talk* describes an action but is also a noun; any native English speaker knows, however, that *talk* is a less formal word than *speech* in modern English. If I give a talk or give a speech, you'll have different ideas in your mind about the nature of my presentation. Here's what this means:

1. Words are difficult to translate from one language to another, because it is impossible for one word to accurately sum up the sense of another word in another language.
2. If you want to get the full sense of a word's semantic range, you need to see the different ways it is used in a language. You need context.

So how is love talked about in the Bible?

LOVE IN THE BIBLE

The Old Testament was written in Hebrew,[5] and one of the Hebrew words that is often translated as "love" in our English Bibles is a Hebrew word we can spell out as *khesed* in English. It's pronounced with a guttural clearing-of-the-throat sound at the beginning of the word, and its second syllable rhymes with the word *bed*. *Khesed* is a difficult word to translate into English because we don't have one single English word that fully captures its semantic range. In Hebrew, *khesed* means something like "generosity / loyalty / steadfast promise-keeping / long-suffering kindness." And how is this beautiful word used? In the Old Testament, *khesed* is most often used to describe God.

The central passage in the Torah that gives insight into God's character is found in Exodus 34. In the background of this passage, the Lord has brought the Israelites out of Egypt to the foot of Mount Sinai. He has made a covenant with them and given them the Ten Commandments. But while Moses is on the mountain receiving further instruction from the Lord, the people immediately break the commandment against idolatry by making a golden calf to worship! Instead of understandably abandoning the people to their idolatry, however, the Lord remains faithful to his promises, and this is because covenant faithfulness is part of who the Lord *is*. As the Lord renews his commitment to the people in front of Moses on Mount Sinai, he provides a remarkable self-revelation: "And he passed in front of Moses, proclaiming, 'The LORD, the LORD, the compassionate and gracious God, slow to anger, abounding in *love* and faithfulness, maintaining *love* to thousands, and forgiving wickedness, rebellion and sin. Yet he does not leave the guilty unpunished; he punishes the children and their children for the sin of the parents to the third and fourth generation'" (Ex. 34:6–7, emphases added).

These three verses are then quoted and referenced more than twenty additional times in the Bible. Why? Because they provide a beautiful insight into and summary of God's character. What's interesting, however, is that the translators of the New International Version have chosen in this passage to translate the Hebrew word *khesed* as "love."

I do not think it is wrong to translate *khesed* this way, but I do think it can be unhelpful for modern people. This is because *love* is too narrow a term for us in modern English, even with *steadfast* as a modifier, as in the English Standard Version. What the underlying word conveys about God is a whole wheelbarrow's worth of meaning: "generosity / loyalty / steadfast promise-keeping / long-suffering kindness." In English, we might hear the plain, sentimental English word *love*, but much more is implied when God is described as showing *khesed*. And this understanding makes a big difference when a later biblical author famously states that "God is love" (1 John 4:8). If what we have in our minds when we think of the love of God is something similar to what Tom Hanks's character shows atop the Empire State Building on Valentine's Day at the end of *Sleepless in Seattle*, then we might be left with a weak, sentimental, and superficial idea of love. No, the way the Lord describes himself is broader and stronger: The love of God is a long-suffering commitment to another's goodness, show-ing kindness and generosity toward that person, even when it costs. I wish there were another, better word for love in modern English, but there isn't. So if we want to understand love in biblical terms, we need to continually have in our minds how it is actually used and expressed in the Bible. We need to know the context—God *is* love.

GOD *IS* LOVE

In the biblical account, we know what love is by looking at God—love is defined by God himself, as something he is. This means that love is primary in its essence—that is to say, it comes first, because God is always first. The first line of the Bible makes it clear: There is God, and then there is everything else: "In the beginning God created the heavens and the earth" (Gen. 1:1). Or as the Nicene Creed affirms:

> We believe in one God,
> the Father, the Almighty,
> maker of heaven and earth,
> of all that is,
> seen and unseen.

God is on one side of the equation, and everything else is on the other side, "seen and unseen." And because God is love, and because all things were created by God, then all things were created by love, and love is a gift that the creation receives from its creator.

To say that God is love is to say that under reality itself, there is love, upholding and sustaining everything. The life of God is a life of love. The British theologian Michael Reeves has some helpful reflections on the implications of the idea that God is love. As he writes in his book *Delighting in the Trinity*,

> The love at the beating heart of reality is the life shared between the Father, Son, and Holy Spirit. God's innermost being . . . is an outgoing, loving, life-giving being. The triune God is an ecstatic God: he is not a God who hoards his life, but one who gives it away, as he would show in that supreme moment of his self-revelation on the cross. The Father finds his very identity in giving his life and being to the Son; and the Son images his Father in sharing his life with us through the Spirit.[6]

God is love and God precedes all things, so that means that love is not first of all a reaction but always something that comes first. "This means," Michael Reeves writes, "that Christ loves the church first and foremost: his love is not a response, given only when the church loves him; his love comes first, and we only love him because he first loved us (1 John 4:19)."[7] Further, because human beings are created by God, love comes to us from outside of us. It is something that originates with God. Love, in the biblical sense, comes from God and does not depend on anything else. This is because the very life of God is a life of love.

Love, then, is not a reaction, it is not a secondary response like an emotion—no, love precedes, it comes first. And this idea of love is exactly the opposite of how the world understands it.

HOW THE WORLD UNDERSTANDS LOVE IS EXACTLY WRONG

The operating definition of love in modern America is that love is a feeling, a response. If I feel lovingly toward someone, then I love that person. Love, therefore, in the worldly understanding, is dependent not on the agent who loves but on the object and its worthiness of being loved. You can diagram this understanding of love like this:

One Who Loves → Loves → Object That Is Worthy

In this definition the object of love *draws* love out of the agent or subject. It might therefore be better to turn the diagram around.

Object That Is Worthy ← Evokes Love in,
Draws Love out of ← The One Who Loves

So when I look at my daughter, she evokes love in me and I love her. Again, love is something I either feel or do not feel because of the thing I am considering. If the thing is worthy, then I love the object of my love. In the world's way of understanding love, love is primarily reactive. Someone strikes me as being worth loving, and I react by loving that person. Whether most Americans would consciously define love in this way is not the point; the point is that what we might call "reactive love" is our culture's working definition of love.

Let's consider the implications of understanding love as being primarily reactive. Imagine a young Hollywood starlet whose good looks make her attractive—people are drawn to her. She is loved because she—according to cultural standards—is worth loving. The lesson to her is clear: To be loved, other people must find you worth loving. What happens when she begins to show signs of aging? She does whatever she can to cover up those signs—if she loses her beauty, she loses any chance of being loved. And so she's driven to more and more desperate measures to try to overcome the natural process of getting older. Living with the world's definition of love is like living in a prison—you are imprisoned by your need to constantly prove that you are worthy of being loved.

Recently I watched an episode of the 1950s television show *Leave It to Beaver* in which the older brother, Wally, makes the baseball team, earning obvious admiration from his father, Ward. The younger brother, Beaver, isn't good enough to play for the team, and though he isn't good enough to play in the school orchestra either, he tries to trick his parents into believing he joined the orchestra because he wants his father to show him the same admiration and approval that Mr. Cleaver shows Wally. *Leave It to Beaver* is a sweet show, and everything works out in the end of the episode and everyone learns a valuable lesson. The world's definition of love is everywhere, and that definition is that love is something you deserve if you're worthy and something you do not deserve if you're not.

The Bible's understanding of love is exactly opposite to that of the world.

If God is love, then any working definition of love we use must conform to what the Bible says about God. What the Bible shows is a God who is constantly pouring out himself for the good of his world. Since this is the case, I think the best working definition of love I have ever come across was provided by the medieval philosopher Thomas Aquinas, who said, "To love is to will the good of the other."[8]

What's useful about this definition is that it removes love from both the realm of the erotic as well as that of the emotional. Despite what the pop culture teaches, if most people think about it for a moment, they will readily concede that love is not exclusively or even primarily erotic. After all, we still have many relationships in our lives in which we love people in a nonsexual way. But even if they agree that love is not exclusively erotic, many people today still mistakenly believe that love is primarily emotional, something one feels. As Aquinas so helpfully puts it, love is properly understood not as a feeling but rather as a commitment to action on another's behalf, something one does, an act initiated by one party for the good of the other party. Because love comes first as an act of the will, it does not depend on the object of the love being worthy or deserving. If that were the case, we could never truly love people we did not feel like loving. This is a vital insight, because otherwise it would be impossible to love someone who was wrong and—more important—it would mean that God would not be able to love sinners. If love is primarily an emotion I feel toward someone, then the only way I can love someone who has wronged me or who is my enemy is by first twisting up my emotions and convincing myself that I somehow feel love toward this person who has hurt and wronged me. But if love is a choice, an action, then new possibilities are opened up.

So I look at my daughter and I love her, irrespective of anything she does or is—I love her because I am her father. Period. She does not have to do anything for me to love her; I love her because I have decided that I will love her. Furthermore, if love is an act of the will, independent of how I feel about someone, then it *is* actually possible for me to love someone I don't really like all that much, someone I do not agree with, even someone who is wrong. This is because my choice to love is not about the object of my love but about me, the subject of the loving act. I can love my enemy while still believing he is my enemy. This biblical understanding of love is fundamentally different from our cultural idea of love. You might even say these two ideas of love are moving in opposite directions.

The World's Idea of Love:

**Object That Is Worthy ← Evokes Love In,
Draws Love out of ← The One Who Loves**

The Bible's Idea of Love:

The One Who Loves → Loves → Irrespective
of Whether the Object Deserves It

I believe this difference—between the world's idea of love and the Bible's idea of love—is at the root of some of our bitterest and most hurtful culture-war arguments, particularly in the disagreements Christians and non-Christians have over questions of human sexuality.

WHY SO MUCH OF THE DEBATE OVER SEXUALITY IS REALLY A DEBATE OVER LOVE (BUT NOT IN THE WAY YOU'RE THINKING)

So often these days, the discussion around anything regarding human sexuality is emotionally charged and painful. Part of the problem is that this debate is typically a disagreement between fundamentally irreconcilable ideas. I'll call them idea A and idea B.

- Idea A: We are defined by our desires, and if we refuse to fully affirm others' desires, we essentially refuse to allow them to exist or deny their personhood and dignity.
- Idea B: We are defined by God's image (in which we were created), and we all need God to save us from our disordered desires.

Now, many disagreements we have with others are not irreconcilable. It is a cliché that happens to be true: Often if we just listen to each other, we can find common ground. But the disagreements people have today about sexuality rarely fit into this category. They aren't about two flavors of the same thing; rather, they are about two different things, two opposite ideas about the human person. At heart, arguments about human sexuality are debates about anthropology—about what it means to be human. But even that doesn't explain why this discussion gets so heated. After all, there are many people I coexist with in this world whose ideas are irreconcilable with mine, and it is sometimes possible to make a kind of cease-fire with people who think completely differently than us so that we can live alongside each other in peace. But something about sexuality seems to make coexistence difficult and the argument particularly bitter. The reason for this is because the sexuality debate is really a debate over the nature of love.

As I mentioned, two irreconcilable ideas are at play: Idea A is how the world thinks of a human being, and idea B is how the church sees the human being. The debate typically goes something like this:

- The church says to the world, "Because we know idea B to be true, we believe you are wrong, but we love you anyway."
- The world replies, "You cannot actually love us because you believe that we who subscribe to idea A are wrong. According to how we understand love, it is impossible to

love people who are wrong, and therefore you do not love us; in fact, you hate us."

This is why the sexuality debate ends up being so bitter. We are working from different definitions of love. The world does not believe you can love someone you also believe is wrong. And this is why so many people are so hard-hearted and hurting: They believe that unless other people find them worthy of being loved, then they will not be loved. Living with this idea is like living in a prison. And God wants to kick down that prison door.

GOD LOVES PEOPLE EVEN
WHEN THEY ARE WRONG

See, the very heart of the gospel is that God loves people even when they are wrong. As the most famous verse in the Scripture puts it: "For God so loved the world that he gave his one and only Son, that whoever believes in him shall not perish but have eternal life" (John 3:16). But it is the often-overlooked next verse in John's gospel that really fleshes out the meaning of what Jesus is saying: "For God did not send his Son into the world to condemn the world, but to save the world through him" (v. 17). Though the world has rejected God, he still moves toward the world in love. As Christians, we should never get over our wonder at the sheer strangeness of this idea. In his letter to the Romans, the apostle Paul expresses astonishment that Jesus would die for people who are actively in sin: "You see, at just the right time, when we were still powerless, Christ died for the ungodly. Very rarely will anyone die for a righteous person, though for a good person someone might possibly dare to die. But God demonstrates his own love for us in this: While we were still sinners, Christ died for us" (Rom. 5:6–8). Or, as the communion liturgy at our church proclaims every week, "Christ died for us while we were yet sinners, which proves God's love toward us."

The love of God moves toward a world that does not deserve it. God loves this world not because the world evokes love in God but because God *is* love. The heartbreaking tragedy that the Bible tells is that humanity, in its rebellion against God, does not understand God's love. From the moment Adam and Eve hid in the garden after their disobedience, right down to the present day, the world believes that God wants only to condemn. This is why judgment alone does not provoke the world to repentance: Because the world does not understand love, the world will never know the love of God unless God's people share it and proclaim it. The world could never have conceived that God would love sinners while they were still sinning. And yet that is love. Love has nothing to do with the recipient of that love, but everything to do with the giver. Love is a choice one makes to will the other's good. Jesus chose to die to free humanity from sin and death and bring us back to God. The world does not have to continue in the way that leads to death; if it would just turn and repent and believe, it would receive the life that Jesus offers. This is the situation in which we find ourselves.

Love, then, is not primarily erotic, nor is love primarily emotional. Instead, love is first and foremost an act of the will. It involves willing the good for another person. According to the Bible, the Lord is best described by this understanding of love—initiating and acting for the good of another. God *is* love, which means that at the heart of reality itself is a beating heart of love—or, to put it another way, underneath everything that is, there God is, willing and working for the utmost good of all. And according to Jesus, the most important thing any of us can ever do is to learn to love in the same way: Love God, and love your neighbor as yourself.

Aquinas says that to love is to will the good of the other. But what does it mean to will the good of someone? The highest good is to know and live in the love of God, knowing God and being known by him. Because the beating heart of reality is the love that the Father, the Son, and the Holy Spirit share with one another, the highest good is to be in relationship with them by accepting the gospel invitation to live in the presence of their love. The Son wants to bring us into this community to experience the love he receives from the Father, and the Father wants to pour out on us the love he has for the Son, and the Spirit is the very love they share that overflows and comes to dwell within us. Salvation is our incorporation into this relationship. The highest good we can will for someone else is that he or she experiences this love. To put it another way, when we play our part in the Great Commission, we are loving our neighbors in the best way possible by telling them about the love of God that has come to us in Christ Jesus our Lord.

Love is never primarily about the object of that love but rather about the subject, the one who loves. God does not love the sinful world because the world deserves that love. In truth, the world does not deserve that love. Rather, God loves the sinful world because God is love. Love is always moving outward from the one who loves toward the object of that love.

WHAT IT MEANS TO SAY THAT
LOVE GOES FIRST

Writer Andy Crouch has spoken of three revolutions that created the modern world. The first was the financial revolution, by which wealth was transferred from land to money. The second was the industrial revolution, by which work moved from being done by bodies—human bodies and animal bodies—to machines. The third is the information revolution, by which knowledge shifted from being about wisdom passed down from the previous generations, person to person, to being about information, accessible in an entirely different and impersonal way.

> The primary obvious result of these three revolutions has been unbelievable prosperity. . . . They've generated untold wealth—in many ways untold health, length of life, quality of life.
>
> But this prosperity has come with a price. We have gained power but lost a sense of our personhood.

142

In the midst of all this abundance and prosperity there seems to be something not quite right. . . . I wonder if what's going on in all three of these revolutions is a kind of trade of personhood for power, which is to say that as we went through these revolutions, we replaced a personal form of human engagement with the world and human actualization in the world with an impersonal form that is far more powerful. . . . The story of the late modern world is the trade of personhood for power . . . and this leads to . . . understand[ing] the great paradox of our time: the great abundance and prosperity [that is all around us] and yet the great sense of dis-ease. . . . Modernity is a great place to have power; it's not a great place to be a person.

Every single person you have ever seen was created in the image of God. This means that every single person you have ever seen is immeasurably valuable, because he or she was created by God. But these priceless creatures are also desperately vulnerable—a human being needs to feel valued in order to thrive.

Every one of us came into the world looking for one thing: The moment we were born, we were looking for a face. We were born and in the shock and surprise of birth we opened our eyes and we looked for a face, because until we see a face—until another sees us—we do not know who we are, and we looked for someone who would look at us. . . . Every human being . . . is looking for someone who is looking for us. We're in this room because someone, some face found our face and locked eyes with us and we were given a name, but at some point in every human life the gaze shifts, the face disappears, no one is looking for us—that's loneliness; and in some lives that happens very early, even just in the moments after birth as a glance is given [and nothing more].[9]

In the garden of Eden, the man and the woman were perfectly valued because they lived in trusting relationship with God. The human is like the sunflower—it needs to face the light. Without the light of God—when we turn aside in rebellion—life becomes burdensome and bitter. Since the sin in the garden of Eden and their exile from Eden, human beings have been desperate to get back to and receive the validating love of God, even if they do not know they need it. To put it another way, every human being is desperate to be seen.

Even the tiniest newborn wants to be seen and known. And though we grow and mature, we never grow beyond that need. One of the tragedies of the modern world is that, despite our great material prosperity, our fundamental need to be seen and known still goes unmet. Though, to paraphrase Crouch, our exchange of personhood for power has made us wealthy, our great wealth has not satisfied our fundamental need to be loved.

What people are looking for is not just acknowledgment—not merely to be seen—but to be seen and known. People do not want merely to be tolerated or pleasantly and politely acknowledged. What every single person truly wants is to be preferred. People are desperate to feel that you are glad they exist. Even if most people cannot articulate this desperation, it is there.

This is what it means to go first in love: to move toward another person in such a way that communicates, "I'm grateful that you are alive and that I get to see you." To move toward another in this way is a pure act of love, because to be seen and known is what every person ultimately needs, and when we move toward another in this way, we are acting in accordance with the will of God. Every time someone acts in this way, the world changes. The world is desperate for God's love even as it pushes God away in sinful idolatry and rebellion. Moving toward another person shares with them the love that comes from God.

We love because God first loved us.

When we move in love toward another person, we are acting in accordance with how God made the world and how he continues to sustain and love a world in rebellion against him. When we go first, we are swimming with the current of the great river of the love of God. To love in this way is to experience God's life, since we are doing what God made us to do, in the way he made us to do it—to love others.

Love goes. It moves toward the other. It does not wait to see how it will be received. It does not give itself only to those who deserve it. Therefore, true love always requires sacrifice—it is costly. When we move first in love, we risk rejection. Love is a free gift, given over completely to the recipient with no guarantee of it being returned. The person who receives love is free to reject it or waste it or abuse it. When you love, you give as a free gift, in grace, and though the gift must be freely given—or it is not a gift—it still costs to give it. More than that, because to love is to will the good of the other, when you love you are giving of yourself for the other's good; the other's good comes at the cost of your own. To put the other before yourself is a costly act, and this is why true love always requires sacrifice.

But love is never, ever wasted. Love does not entropy or fall apart; rather, "love never fails" (1 Cor. 13:8). When we move toward another in love, reality is permanently changed—whether or not the other receives or acknowledges our love or wastes our love. The fact that the Father sent the Son to die for the world has changed reality forever, whether or not the world acknowledges that gift. Love always changes things.

All of this is summed up in the three-word theme of this book, three words to live by and three words that can change the world: *Love goes first.*

Once you see it, you see it everywhere.

DISCUSSION QUESTIONS

1. Have you ever considered the rules of a game to be a form of love? What happens if you try to play without rules?
2. Why does the psalmist rejoice over God's law?
3. Are rules easier to follow if we know the intention behind them?
4. How does Thomas Aquinas's definition of love change how you think of the love of God?

5. How would it affect a marriage if one of the spouses lived by the world's definition of love?

6. Why are our arguments over human sexuality so bitter?

7. How does the world's definition of love imprison the people who live by it?

6

GOING FIRST IN THE WORD AND IN THE WORLD

God is love and he has woven love into the universe itself. When we go first in love, we are merely moving in accordance with the way God made the world to work. Since this is true, then, it should not surprise us to see examples all around us of how love goes first.

We love because he first loved us.
—1 JOHN 4:19

Candice Marie Benbow had the worst kind of neighbor one could have in a New York City apartment building—one who blasts electronic dance music from dusk till dawn. After a particularly bad night before Christmas—music blaring until 4:00 a.m.—she reached her breaking point. Does one bang on the door and say, "Turn it off!"? Call the police? Buy a powerful subwoofer, place it against the adjoining wall, turn it to eleven, and try to defeat his noise, decibel for decibel, with a thumping bass line of one's own? No, what Candice Benbow did was bake a pound cake, write a letter, and leave it on her neighbor's doorstep. And then she waited.

The cake was a peace offering, and the letter was a firm but funny and polite request that he turn down his music. Later, the cake and the letter were gone. That next night, the music was lower than it had ever been. Three days later they actually met—he wanted to thank her for the pound cake. It turned out that the neighbor was a music video producer who was about to experience Christmas for the first time since his daughter had died in a car accident.[1]

The argument of this book is that if you want to change the world, you have to go first, because love goes first. When you go first in love, you change the relational dynamic. We have discussed what love is and why—in an age that prioritizes feelings over facts, in a world divided by fears and enmities—often the only way to break through is to drop your guard, take the risk, and move toward the other. This move is so unexpected that it often upends the status quo and makes a new reality possible. It's the ping-pong player hitting a shot that her opponent never thought possible, or the fighter pilot pushing his plane into a maneuver that no one in his right mind would ever dream of making. Going first scrambles things. But in a good way.

But because going first is such a strange thing to do, the more we can see examples of it, the better we can understand and identify opportunities to make the first move in our own lives. Fortunately, examples abound, both within the Bible and within the world.

The reason why examples of love going first are every-where is because God has woven love into the fabric of reality. God is love and so when reality was created, it was created with love. You do not need a PhD in physics to be able to ride a bike; you do not need to understand how a bicycle moves in order to ride off on two wheels. But even if you do not know the under-lying principles of bicycle riding, it is also the case that if you are going to ride a bike, you cannot work against those prin-ciples. In the same way, whether we are aware of it or not, love is how reality works. Love is the direction things are moving. So whether or not we know it, when we move toward another in love, we are swimming with the current. Even before people knew about the law of gravity, they knew how to work with it. In the same way, it should not surprise us to find examples all around us of how love goes first.

We see this in the Bible, which is a metanarrative of God's going first in love. From the creation of light on the first page to the light of the Lord himself shining and eradicating the darkness on the last page, God is always moving first in love toward his creation. The act that brings the rebellious cosmos back to God is the ultimate act of going first in love—the incarnation. Love is the unifying story of Scripture, and the sacrifice Jesus made to save the world is woven into the biblical story, from first to last.

THE REUNIFICATION OF THE SONS OF JACOB

The question that the latter part of the book of Genesis wrestles with is this: Who will lead the family after the patriarch Jacob dies? Jacob has twelve sons, and a jealous feud among the brothers results in Joseph—their father's favorite and the second-youngest of the brothers—being sold into Egyptian slavery, despite being only seventeen years old. The ten older brothers[2] lie to their father and tell him that Joseph has been killed by a wild animal. But God is with Joseph in the years of his exile in Egypt, and as the decades pass, he is raised to prominence in Pharaoh's palace.

Meanwhile, years later famine comes to the family in the land of Canaan. So Jacob sends the remaining sons away to buy grain from Egypt. While there, they encounter Joseph, who immediately knows them, even though they do not recognize him. Joseph, who is undeniably brilliant, puts into motion an elaborate scheme to get his brothers to face their guilt for selling him decades before. It is clear that, at this point in the narrative, Joseph has no interest in forgiveness. The scheme culminates with Joseph having a silver cup planted in his youngest brother's luggage, thereby giving Joseph a pretense to detain him. This entrapment provides Joseph a chance to test his brothers. Will they leave their youngest brother to rot in prison? Or have they changed from the days when they sold their brother Joseph into slavery?

The fourth brother, Judah, has emerged as one of the potential candidates for leadership in the family. When confronted with the crisis of his little brother Benjamin being falsely detained, Judah shows something that wasn't there before. His actions at this point in the narrative ensure that he will be the one to lead the family after the patriarch Jacob has died, and that Judah—the fourth son—will be the one from whom future leaders and kings of Israel will descend.

Rather than abandoning his brother—as he did before—Judah steps up and offers himself in Benjamin's place.

When Judah and his brothers came to Joseph's house, he was still there. They fell before him to the ground. Joseph said to them, "What deed is this that you have done? Do you not know that a man like me can indeed practice divination?" And Judah said, "What shall we say to my lord? What shall we speak? Or how can we clear ourselves? God has found out the guilt of your servants; behold, we are my lord's servants, both we and he also in whose hand the cup has been found." But he said, "Far be it from me that I should do so! Only the man in whose hand the cup was found shall be my servant. But as for you, go up in peace to your father."

Then Judah went up to him and said, "Oh, my lord, please let your servant speak a word in my lord's ears, and let not your anger burn against your servant, for you are like Pharaoh himself. My lord asked his servants, saying, 'Have you a father, or a brother?' And we said to my lord, 'We have a father, an old man, and a young brother, the child of his old age. His brother is dead, and he alone is left of his mother's children, and his father loves him.' Then you said to your servants, 'Bring him down to me, that I may set my eyes on him.' We said to my lord, 'The boy cannot leave his father, for if he should leave his father, his father would die.' Then you said to your servants, 'Unless your youngest brother comes down with you, you shall not see my face again.'

"When we went back to your servant my father, we told him the words of my lord. And when our father said, 'Go again, buy us a little food,' we said, 'We cannot go down. If our youngest brother goes with us, then we will go down. For we cannot see the man's face unless our youngest brother is with us.' Then your servant my father said to us, 'You know that my wife bore me two sons. One left me, and I said, "Surely he has been torn to pieces," and I have never seen him since. If you take this one also from me, and harm happens to him, you will bring down my gray hairs in evil to Sheol.'

"Now therefore, as soon as I come to your servant my father, and the boy is not with us, then, as his life is bound up in the boy's life, as soon as he sees that the boy is not with us, he will die, and your servants will bring down the gray hairs of your servant our father with sorrow to Sheol. *For your servant became a pledge of safety for the boy to my father, saying, 'If I do not bring him back to you, then I shall bear the blame before my father all my life.'* Now therefore, please let your servant remain instead of the boy as a servant to my lord, and let the boy go back with his brothers. For how can I go back to my father if the boy is not with me? I fear to see the evil that would find my father."

—GENESIS 44:14–34 ESV, EMPHASIS ADDED

This is the longest speech in Genesis, and one of the longest in the entire Bible. It's a beautiful statesmanlike speech, moving in its raw, honest emotion. And it is these words that finally pierce through Joseph's carefully guarded exterior and break his heart. Judah puts himself forward as a pledge of safety, agreeing to bear the blame should any harm fall upon him. His commitment is to his brother's good, even at the cost of his own life. The one who had sold his brother into slavery is now humbled, willing to give his life to preserve that of his youngest brother. Judah, not willing that others should suffer, goes first and offers himself in his brother's place. Judah's sacrifice is what finally breaks through Joseph's hard heart and reunites the brothers.

Then Joseph could not control himself before all those who stood by him. He cried, "Make everyone go out from me." So no one stayed with him when Joseph made himself known to his brothers. And he wept aloud, so that the Egyptians heard it, and the household of Pharaoh heard it. And Joseph said to his brothers, "I am Joseph! Is my father still alive?" But his brothers could not answer him, for they were dismayed at his presence.

So Joseph said to his brothers, "Come near to me, please." And they came near. And he said, "I am your brother, Joseph, whom you sold into Egypt. And now do not be distressed or angry with yourselves because you sold me here, for God sent me before you to preserve life." . . . And he kissed all his brothers and wept upon them. After that his brothers talked with him.

—GENESIS 45:1–5, 15 ESV

In one of the great scenes of the Bible, we witness the reunification of the sons of Jacob. And how are they reunited? By Judah's commitment at any cost to move first and sacrifice himself for his brother. Decades before, the sons of Jacob had decided to kill their obnoxious and brilliant brother Joseph, the eleventh son and their father's favorite in his many-colored coat. Judah, to his credit, spoke up at the time and suggested that the brothers make a profit by selling Joseph into slavery instead of killing him, and in the providence of God this is the course they chose, dooming Joseph to years of slavery and imprisonment before the Lord arranged for Joseph's rise to power and prominence. Now, in a great reversal, an act of sacrificial love covers over the former sin, making a way for the betrayed brother to save his former enemies and reunite his family. Judah's sacrifice opens up a possibility whereby Joseph becomes the deliverer of his family.

Joseph has never forgotten that his own brothers sold him into slavery. Can you imagine the screams of the teenage Joseph when the older brothers threw him into the pit and then, after callously deliberating, sold him to the slave traders? I imagine the memory of those terrible moments haunted Joseph for the rest of his life. Now, decades later, seeing the willing sacrifice of Judah—one of the brothers who was so hard-hearted toward him before—he weeps so loudly that his Egyptian servants in other parts of the house can hear it. He reveals himself to his stupefied brothers and requests that they bring their elderly father, Jacob, down to Egypt.

Judah's is a powerful example of love in action, of love going first by sacrificing for the sake of another. We see this pattern throughout the Scriptures, even when the one who goes first would rather die than see his enemies blessed.

JONAH: THE UNHAPPIEST SUCCESSFUL MISSIONARY OF ALL TIME

We find another story of going first in the strange little story of Jonah the prophet. The word of the Lord comes to Jonah telling him that he is to go and preach repentance to the Ninevites, the hated enemies of Israel. As we read in Revelation, we know that judgment is coming for those who refuse to acknowledge God as Lord. The same was true in the time of Jonah. As the word of the Lord comes to Jonah at the beginning of the book, we learn that if the Ninevites do not repent, it will soon be too late. The situation is urgent, for unless someone tells the Ninevites that the Lord does not desire their destruction but wants to offer them life, these lost people will never know about the grace of God.

So there is hope for the Ninevites, and the Lord sends Jonah to Nineveh as a messenger of grace to share the good news with them. The problem is that Nineveh is the capital city of the wicked Assyrian Empire, the great enemy of Israel. The Assyrian army murdered and tortured the Israelites and the Assyrians were widely known and feared for their cruelty. Because of their wickedness—and especially their wickedness toward his own people—Jonah does not want the Ninevites to repent, because he does not want them to be saved. Jonah is being asked to work for the good of the Ninevites, but their good is exactly what Jonah does not want. Instead, Jonah wants the Ninevites to face judgment for their wickedness, but he has been asked by God to set aside his desire for revenge and instead to will their good so they will hear God's word, repent, and receive God's mercy. Love always comes with a cost, and for Jonah the cost that comes with loving his enemies is one he does not want to pay.

Jonah, it will turn out, is not so much afraid of his enemies the Ninevites as he is afraid that the Lord will be merciful to them!³ Jonah is loath to be the means by which the mercy of God comes to his enemies. This is why he tries to flee in the opposite direction, but the Lord famously blocks his flight over the sea and forces him back to Nineveh. Eventually, Jonah reluctantly goes to the city of his enemies and preaches the need for repentance, delivering what is perhaps the shortest and most passive-aggressive sermon in history: "Jonah obeyed the word of the LORD and went to Nineveh. Now Nineveh was a very large city; it took three days to go through it. Jonah began by going a day's journey into the city, proclaiming, 'Forty more days and Nineveh will be overthrown'" (Jonah 3:3–4).

One has the impression of Jonah barely putting his foot inside the city gates before delivering his prophetic message as quickly as possible, like some kind of verbal hot potato. Regardless of the reluctance of the minister, however, Jonah's ministry is immediately and miraculously successful—the entire city repents!

> The Ninevites believed God. A fast was proclaimed, and all of them, from the greatest to the least, put on sackcloth.
>
> When Jonah's warning reached the king of Nineveh, he rose from his throne, took off his royal robes, covered himself with sackcloth and sat down in the dust. This is the proclamation he issued in Nineveh:
>
> "By the decree of the king and his nobles:
>
> Do not let people or animals, herds or flocks, taste anything; do not let them eat or drink. But let people and animals be covered with sackcloth. Let everyone call

urgently on God. Let them give up their evil ways and their violence. Who knows? God may yet relent and with compassion turn from his fierce anger so that we will not perish."

When God saw what they did and how they turned from their evil ways, he relented and did not bring on them the destruction he had threatened.

—JONAH 3:5–10

Jonah, an enemy of Assyria, goes to the Assyrian capital city and proclaims a message of repentance *and it works.* Although he is an unwilling messenger, nevertheless Jonah does in fact move toward the Ninevites, and his action creates the environment in which they are able and willing to hear about the grace of God. The sight of an Israelite coming to their city and warning the Ninevites that it is not too late for them to avoid their looming destruction is a sight that breaks through their hard hearts and opens them up to hearing God's word. All it took was someone going to them and showing them what the love of God is like.[4]

THE TIME JESUS INVITED
HIMSELF TO DINNER

What Judah and Jonah and the others are doing—though they do not know it—is foreshadowing the greatest example of God's love in the Bible, the incarnation. The entire ministry of Jesus was one of moving first toward sinners, and that move

161

began in the manger. God comes to us, as even the prophetic name of Jesus makes clear: "All this took place to fulfill what the Lord had said through the prophet: 'The virgin will conceive and give birth to a son, and they will call him Immanuel' (which means 'God with us')" (Matt. 1:22–23). Jesus described his work as that of going to people who were sick, not healthy: "It is not the healthy who need a doctor, but the sick. I have not come to call the righteous, but sinners to repentance" (Luke 5:31–32). In Jesus, the love of God moves toward a world that does not deserve it.

In an earlier chapter, we saw how Jesus moved first toward the Samaritan woman—"Can I have some water?"—an act that upended the status quo and caused her to be open to a new spiritual possibility. The Samaritan woman was an outsider, but Jesus follows the same strategy with Jews as well. Consider, for example, his interaction with Zacchaeus the tax collector (Luke 19:1–10).

> Jesus entered Jericho and was passing through. A man was there by the name of Zacchaeus; he was a chief tax collector and was wealthy. He wanted to see who Jesus was, but because he was short he could not see over the crowd. So he ran ahead and climbed a sycamore-fig tree to see him, since Jesus was coming that way.

In the time of Jesus, the Romans employed a system of taxation called tax farming, whereby they gave out licenses that enabled the license holder to collect as many taxes as possible.

As long as he paid the Romans the appropriate amount, a tax farmer could pocket the rest of what he collected. It was a system open to abuse. Is Zacchaeus boxed out by the crowd because he is short, or are they turning their backs on him because of his collaboration with the hated Roman oppressors? Zacchaeus knows he is a sinner, everyone else knows he is a sinner, and Zacchaeus knows that everyone else knows he is a sinner.

Which is why what Jesus does is so surprising:

> When Jesus reached the spot, he looked up and said to him, "Zacchaeus, come down immediately. I must stay at your house today." So he came down at once and welcomed him gladly.
>
> All the people saw this and began to mutter, "He has gone to be the guest of a sinner."

Everyone knows that what Jesus has done is strange. For Jesus to have dinner with someone as notorious as Zacchaeus was to convey an honor on Zacchaeus that he definitely did not merit. The crowd is scandalized. And yet there is a method to Jesus' madness, because the very act that troubles the crowd is the act that breaks through and provokes the little wicked man to repentance:

> But Zacchaeus stood up and said to the Lord, "Look, Lord! Here and now I give half of my possessions to the poor, and if I have cheated anybody out of anything, I will pay back four times the amount."

Jesus said to him, "Today salvation has come to this house, because this man, too, is a son of Abraham. For the Son of Man came to seek and to save the lost."

The reason Zaccheaus is so moved when Jesus peremptorily invites himself to the tax collector's house is because Zacchaeus knows that Jesus knows that how Zaccheaus makes a living is wrong. What Zacchaeus cannot understand is why someone who knew he was wrong would want to spend time with him, and the reverse invitation Jesus gives him becomes a bewildering experience of grace. When someone knows you know and you still go first anyway, you create space for the grace of God to lead someone to repentance.

We see this principle play itself out yet again in perhaps the most famous of all of Jesus' parables, the parable of the prodigal son. The disgraceful wayward son comes to his senses in a foreign land, admits to himself that he is wrong, and forms a plan to head back home and apologize to his father: "When he came to his senses, he said, 'How many of my father's hired servants have food to spare, and here I am starving to death! I will set out and go back to my father and say to him: Father, I have sinned against heaven and against you. I am no longer worthy to be called your son; make me like one of your hired servants.' So he got up and went to his father" (Luke 15:17–20).

While the son has already admitted he has been in the wrong, he also knows he does not deserve a place in the family again. So how does the father's run toward his wayward son change that family's future? "But while he was still a long way off, his father saw him and was filled with compassion for him; he ran to his son, threw his arms around him and kissed him" (v. 20). What if the father had stood on principle and made his son grovel for forgiveness?[5]

The father transgresses a boundary separating him from his son and moves toward him in an utterly surprising way— just as Jesus does with the Samaritan woman ("Can I have a drink?") and with Zaccheaus ("I'm coming to your house for dinner"). In each of these interactions, it is the very fact that the one who goes first is in the right that makes the action so effective. When *they* know that *you* know, and yet you move anyway—that's how to break through.

But breakthroughs are not confined only to the Bible. This is because love is not just the unifying theme of Scripture but the unifying theme of all reality. God has made the world a certain way, and if we choose to work with God—to swim with the current—then we should not be surprised when the one who goes first changes things. Just as in the Bible, examples of what happens when one person chooses to move toward another in love are all around. You just have to know what you're looking for.

OSCAR GRACE

I remember watching the Academy Awards in 2004. Bill Murray—one of my favorite actors—had been nominated for the Best Actor Oscar that year for his movie *Lost in Translation*.

At the Oscars, the camera lingers on the faces of each of the losing nominees after the winner has been announced. Perhaps this reflects our twisted desire to see the pain and disappointment of others. I will never forget seeing Bill Murray look particularly crushed when Sean Penn was announced as the winner that year. Bill likely knew he'd never get back there again, especially because most of his career has been as a comedic actor, not someone who takes on the dramatic roles that typically win awards.

I was reminded of that moment when I saw the award given for Best Director at the 2020 Academy Awards. The Korean director Bong Joon Ho was announced as the winner, and the camera lingered on the faces of the four losing directors: Martin Scorsese, Quentin Tarantino, Sam Mendes, and Todd Phillips. (I thought Mr. Phillips looked particularly disappointed.) Seeing the real-time disappointment on the faces of men who had been working their entire lives to win one of the world's greatest prizes only to be told in front of millions of people that they were unsuccessful made me uncomfortable. Honestly, I felt sorry for them. Can you imagine having your life's greatest disappointments shown in real time around the globe? There is nowhere to hide.

And then I listened as Bong Joon Ho made his speech, and watched how his words changed the atmosphere in the room in a moment. If you haven't seen it, the entire thing is worth watching.[6] Mr. Bong begins by deftly recognizing Martin Scorsese in such a pure and heartfelt way that the entire audience gives *Martin Scorsese* a standing ovation. As the audience stands to its feet and applauds, Mr. Scorsese seems in the moment to be completely caught off guard and humbled in a way that can only ever be spontaneous, never planned. It's as if he feels overwhelmed and undeserving at the goodwill shown to him by his peers. He flashes this beautiful spontaneous smile, bashful and boyish. Then Bong credits Quentin Tarantino with generously promoting his films in America when no one had heard of him, and *then* he tells Todd Phillips and Sam Mendes that he wishes he could cut the Oscar statuette in pieces and share it with them. Mr. Phillips grins, an unguarded and unexpected expression, almost in spite of himself. It's as if grace has been poured out on the entire theater, with everyone just grateful to be there and experience the moment. It's beautiful.

Grace changes everything.

What I found so moving about that Oscar moment is how Bong Joon Ho was willing to go first. He could have offered another obligatory acceptance speech, thanking the usual suspects. Or he could have ranted about his pet project or his political views to virtue signal to the world. Instead, he was able to change the feel of an entire auditorium filled with some of the most self-absorbed, entitled people in the world. Why? Bong made his rivals for the Academy Award—and, through those rivals, the audience in that room and the rest of us watching on television—feel loved, and he made them feel wanted.

And that's what people want more than anything—to feel wanted. Just ask Jerry Jones and Jimmy Johnson.

THE RING OF HONOR: WHAT DO YOU GET
THE BILLIONAIRE WHO HAS EVERYTHING?

Jerry Jones came to town and made an immediate splash. A self-described oil wildcatter and good ol' boy from Arkansas, Jerry—everyone always calls him Jerry—made a fortune in oil and proceeded to buy the Dallas Cowboys in 1989. One of his first acts was to fire the only coach the Dallas Cowboys had ever had—Tom Landry—and bring in Jimmy Johnson, who had been his teammate at the University of Arkansas. Jerry then hired himself to be the general manager of the Cowboys, a move that is almost unprecedented in professional sports— having the same person being both the owner of the team and the team's general manager. Most owners hire someone else to run their teams, but Jerry wanted to do it himself.

At first the pairing of Jerry and Jimmy (everyone in Dallas always calls him Jimmy) worked perfectly. The Cowboys quickly turned from being one of the worst teams in the league when Jerry bought the team to one of the best, winning back-to-back Super Bowls. But then the tension mounted between GM and coach, with Jerry feeling that Jimmy was getting too much of the credit. At the annual NFL meetings in March 1994, after the Cowboys' second Super Bowl win, Jerry told a reporter, "There are five hundred coaches who could have won the Super Bowl with our team."[7] Jimmy Johnson resigned in fury before the end of the month, and that was the start of a thirty-year feud.

Although the Cowboys went on to win another Super Bowl

without Jimmy, football people like to say it was still the team Jimmy built. And since that 1995 Super Bowl win with the team Jimmy built, the Dallas Cowboys haven't been anywhere close to a championship. Over those thirty years, numerous coaches and players have come and gone, but the general manager has stayed the same—it has always been Jerry as GM.

And it has always been Jerry as owner, which means he has the final say as to which Cowboys player or coach makes it into the Ring of Honor. The Ring of Honor is like a hall of fame for the Dallas Cowboys, and those who are inducted into the Ring of Honor have their names emblazoned in big letters on a large strip of metal that rings the interior of the stadium where the Cowboys play, under one of the main concourses. By any measure, Jimmy Johnson was a worthy candidate for the Ring of Honor—he won two Super Bowls in Dallas! But Jerry Jones refused to drop his feud and let Jimmy in. Three decades passed since they worked together, but still Jerry would not relent.

Until suddenly and surprisingly in November 2023, he did. Jerry surprised Jimmy Johnson on television—Jimmy was working as a studio broadcaster for one of the networks—and told him live on the broadcast that he was going to be inducted into the Cowboys' Ring of Honor. If you watch the video, you will see the camera move in for a close-up on Jimmy as Jerry tells him, "You need to be in the Dallas Cowboys Ring of Honor," and you can immediately see on Jimmy's face what those words, coming from that man, mean to him. Jimmy is eighty years old at the time, but it's a childlike look he flashes in a brief moment of unguarded joy, pleased at being preferred.[8]

The induction took place on December 27, 2023, down on the field at halftime in AT&T Stadium, the Cowboys' home stadium in Arlington, Texas. Jimmy made a speech and got the crowd going, and then he said something very simple: thank you. In front of tens of thousands in the stadium and millions of viewers on live television, he said to Jerry Jones, "I'm so very, very proud. Proud of what we accomplished. When I say 'we,' I mean a lot of people. But more than anyone else, thank you, Jerry Jones, for bringing me to the Dallas Cowboys."[9]

It was a touching moment. Here were two old men who were learning what it takes to be reconciled after three decades of a pointless bitter and prideful feud. Jerry went first and finally invited Jimmy into the Ring of Honor, thereby acknowledging Jimmy's talent and success, and then Jimmy made sure to let everyone know that he owed his position to Jerry, thereby recognizing Jerry's authority and vision.

What do you get the billionaire who has everything?

The feeling of being loved.

THAT HAUNTING COUCH SCENE
IN *AMERICAN BEAUTY*

The 1999 Sam Mendes movie *American Beauty* was a commercial success when it came out, and I remember seeing it in the theater. It was also a critical darling at the time and went on to win a pile of Academy Awards, including Best Picture,

Best Director, and Best Actor for Kevin Spacey, who played the lead role.

I'll be honest with you—I hated *American Beauty* and I do not at all recommend it. If you haven't seen it, don't. But I have to grudgingly give it credit because there is one scene from the movie that I still think about decades later: the scene between the husband and wife on the couch.

The movie shows a bleak picture of family dysfunction. Kevin Spacey's character, Lester, is married to Carolyn, played by Annette Bening. He is an inattentive husband, and she is unfaithful. There is no love in their marriage. One day she comes home from work to find him in their living room. They begin to argue, but it isn't vicious. Then suddenly Lester really looks at his wife, and his tone changes. He says, "Have you done something different? You look great." Immediately it's like the atmosphere in the room has been transformed. Carolyn is taken aback, but pleased. She sits on their fancy couch, and he moves forward, reminding her of what their lives were like when they were much younger and happier. Lester approaches and leans in to kiss her, beer bottle in his hand. There is the feeling of tension about to be released and it's like the audience holds its breath, hoping for a breakthrough. And then the tension snaps as Carolyn says sharply, "Lester, you're going to spill beer on the couch!" He reacts angrily and the moment passes, never to be recovered. There will be no reconciliation, and the plot slides farther toward its dark conclusion.

That scene has stayed with me for twenty-five years. A dead

marriage and two sad people, and then a brief moment when one moves toward the other. All the memories of bitterness are lifted and for a moment it seems possible they could love each other again—and then the possibility dies.

Sometimes the hardest people to move toward in love are those closest to us. These are people with whom we have history, and people who know how to hurt us should they choose to do so. And yet in those closest relationships, going first can have profound effects. My wife and I have not had too many bitter fights in our marriage, but we have had a few. Every now and then we will go to bed angry, unwilling to reconcile. I don't like to think about those times because the memory of them makes me sick to my stomach. A few times we have gotten in bed and had our backs turned against each other, unwilling to make even the slightest gesture of reconciliation. I know that in those times all I need to do is turn toward her and apologize, or tell her I don't want to live like this, or otherwise show her I do not want to remain at odds. And yet I will resist reconciliation and stay up long into the night nursing my anger. All the while I am secretly wishing she will reach out to me, as I want the cycle of anger to end, but I'm unwilling to end it myself.

The good news is that God has made the first move toward us. We love because God first loved us (1 John 4:19). Thanks be to God that the Lord did not stand far off, fanning the flames of his righteous anger toward the rebellious world, but rather, because of his *khesed*, he came close. "This is how God showed his love among us: He sent his one and only Son into the world that we might live through him. This is love: not that we loved

God, but that he loved us and sent his Son as an atoning sacrifice for our sins. Dear friends, since God so loved us, we also ought to love one another" (1 John 4:9–11). Every time that we then love in the way God loves, every time we make the first move toward another, a new gracious possibility is opened.

I am aware that many people are in marriages and other relationships with years of hurt in the background, but I also know there is no way for those relationships to be healed without one person making the first move—someone will need to go first and take that initial step toward reconciliation. Sometimes it's as simple as a genuine smile and a simple remark: "Have you done something different? You look great."

At other times it's being the first one to take out your quill pen and write a letter to a fellow signer of the Declaration of Independence.

JULY 4, 1826

Thomas Jefferson and John Adams both died on the fiftieth anniversary of the signing of the Declaration of Independence, July 4, 1826. Jefferson died at Monticello, his Virginia home, at around one o'clock in the afternoon. He was eighty-three years old. That same afternoon, Adams lay on his own deathbed, surrounded by loved ones: "Adams lay peacefully, his mind clear, by all signs. Then late in the afternoon, according to several who were present in the room, he stirred and whispered clearly enough to be understood, 'Thomas Jefferson survives.'"[10]

173

Then a few hours later, at about six-twenty in the evening, John Adams died. He was ninety years old. Both men had lived to see the fiftieth anniversary of the Declaration of Independence, and each man died believing the other still survived. The fact that they both died on the same day is amazing. The fact that they died as friends is a miracle.

Both Adams and Jefferson were relatively young men when they were tasked by the Continental Congress with the writing of the document that would enumerate the reasons the thirteen colonies were declaring their independence from King George—when the Declaration of Independence was signed on July 4, 1776, Adams was forty and Jefferson only thirty-three. Although their signatures on the document prove that they were united in spirit and purpose at that point in their lives, as their long and distinguished careers played out, they became bitter enemies and had no contact with each other for years. Both served as president of the United States, but in rival parties, with Jefferson succeeding Adams to the office—two of the great men of the American Revolution implacably estranged from each other.

Their mutual friend—and signer of the Declaration from Pennsylvania—Dr. Benjamin Rush was grieved at the enmity between Adams and Jefferson and tried for several years to get them to reconcile. Then, in December 1811,

> just before Christmas, Adams heard again from Benjamin Rush who wished to remind him of a visit Adams had had the summer before from two young men from Virginia.

174

They were brothers named Coles, Albemarle County neighbors of Jefferson's, and in the course of conversation Adams had at length exclaimed, "I have always loved Jefferson and I still love him." This had been carried back to Monticello, and was all Jefferson needed to hear. To Rush he wrote, "I only needed this knowledge to revive toward him all the affections of the most cordial moments of our lives."

"And now, my dear friend," declared Rush to Adams, "permit me again to suggest to you to receive the olive branch offered to you by the hand of a man who still loves you."

On New Year's Day 1812, seated at his desk in the second-floor library, Adams took up his pen to write a short letter to Jefferson. . . .

The brief letter from Adams immediately produced a response in Jefferson:

If, as stage-managed by Rush, it had been left to Adams to make the first move, Jefferson more than fulfilled his part. "A letter from you calls up recollections very dear to my mind," he continued. "It carried me back to the times when, beset with difficulties and dangers, we were fellow laborers in the same cause, struggling for what is most valuable to man, his right of self-government."[11]

In the fourteen years that followed their dramatic reconciliation, both men exchanged dozens and dozens of letters on every possible topic. Though they were both old men in those years, they recalled and relived the months and moments of that bright time in their lives, decades before, when they were part of the great events of the American Revolution. Their letters are a precious gift to posterity and part of the inheritance of all subsequent Americans.

They are also a testament to the life-changing power of forgiveness and the catalyzing potential of going first. What if, resisting Dr. Rush's prodding, Adams had refused to send his initial letter to Jefferson? What if Jefferson, nursing decades-old grievances, had refused to reply? I find it fascinating—though not at all surprising—that these great men of American history just needed someone to go first to turn them back toward each other and move them toward reconciliation. They each wanted to be liked by the other. For Jefferson, what moved him was the repetition in his presence of a chance favorable remark Adams had uttered to someone else; for Adams, it was the knowledge that Jefferson still loved him and had said so in a letter to Rush. The whole story is beautiful—a little jewel of American history.

None of it would've been possible without forgiveness.

FIRST TO FORGIVE

On September 6, 2018, a Dallas police officer named Amber Guyger finished her shift and went home to her apartment building, South Side Flats in Dallas, Texas. Each of the floors in South Side Flats looks similar, and in a bizarre series of events, Ms.

Guyger entered the wrong apartment thinking it was hers, saw a man inside, pulled out her service pistol, and killed the man, named Botham Jean, in his own apartment. Guyger is a white woman and was a police officer; Mr. Jean was a black man and an unarmed civilian. The incident drew international attention.

On October 2, 2019, Jean's younger brother, Brandt, delivered a victim impact statement at Guyger's trial. Guyger had just been convicted of Jean's murder. Apparently, Brandt Jean didn't know cameras would record his statement that day; he thought the reporters had already left the Dallas, Texas, courtroom. Here's what this eighteen-year-old young man said to his brother's killer:

> If you truly are sorry, I know I can speak for myself, I forgive you. And I know if you go to God and ask him, he will forgive you.
>
> And I don't think anyone can say it—again I'm speaking for myself and not on behalf of my family—but I love you just like anyone else.
>
> And I'm not going to say I hope you rot and die, just like my brother did, but I personally want the best for you. And I wasn't going to ever say this in front of my family or anyone, but I don't even want you to go to jail. I want the best for you, because I know that's exactly what Botham would want you to do.
>
> And the best would be: give your life to Christ.
>
> I'm not going to say anything else. I think giving your life to Christ would be the best thing that Botham would want you to do.

Again, I love you as a person. And I don't wish anything bad on you.

[Turning and addressing the judge:] I don't know if this is possible, but can I give her a hug, please? Please?[12]

Within a few short hours, that statement had been broadcast around the world.

After Brandt Jean's remarkable statement, the judge granted his heartfelt request to hug Guyger, and he and his brother's killer hugged for a long time in the courtroom while an unidentified woman sobbed in the background. I don't know what life holds for either person, but I am certain of two things: first, that that embrace never would have taken place had not that brave young man chosen first to forgive, and second, that his act of grace in that courtroom changed reality forever. The world is different now because of what Brandt Jean did that day.

As we have seen, if you are willing to make the first move and act rather than wait and react, you will upset the status quo and open up new possibilities. This is true for fighter pilots and it's true for ping-pong players. And it is true for us, too. If we want to overcome division and reach the people who hate us—if the church is going to be obedient to the Great Commission—we are going to have to go first. But that first move, as we have seen in this chapter, is not a first move for control or gain but a first move for the good of the other—it is a way of showing love by moving toward the other, regardless of whether the other is deserving or worthy. This is the basic pattern of reality because God is love, and when we love, we are working with the way the Lord has made the world, swimming with the current of the will of God. This is why going first has such power to change things—when we move toward another in love, it's as if we are tapping into a secret power line that God laid before the foundation of the world.

But going first comes with a cost. The love of God, though freely given, was indescribably costly to give. The same is true for us—yes, going first has the power to change the world, but it is going to cost us everything.

DISCUSSION QUESTIONS

1. How is Judah's decision to offer himself an example of going first in love? What is it about his action that affects Joseph so acutely?

2. Jonah does not want God to be merciful to the Ninevites. What is it about seeing other people receive mercy that can be so difficult?

3. In a close personal relationship—as in a marriage or a family—why is it so hard to be the one who makes the first move?

4. When you choose to forgive, what are you choosing to give up and let go of?

5. Dr. Benjamin Rush played an essential role in the reconciliation between John Adams and Thomas Jefferson. What often holds us back from playing that role in the lives of others?

6. In this chapter we looked at several examples of people going first and thereby changing things for the better. Are there other examples that come to mind?

7. Is there someone in your life who needs to feel loved by you? What might be at stake if you decided to go first toward that person?

7

THE ONLY THING IT TAKES TO GO FIRST IS EVERYTHING

It is important that we are honest with ourselves—to go first will always come with a cost, and it may cost us everything. The good news? God raises the dead and the resurrection is the ultimate vindication: Love wins.

Then Jesus said to his disciples, "Whoever wants to be my disciple must deny themselves and take up their cross and follow me. For whoever wants to save their life will lose it, but whoever loses their life for me will find it. What good will it be for someone to gain the whole world, yet forfeit their soul? Or what can anyone give in exchange for their soul?"
—MATTHEW 16:24–26

On January 8, 1956, Nate Saint landed a little Piper airplane on a sandy river beach deep in the Ecuadorian Amazon. With him were four other American young men—Jim Elliot, Roger Youderian, Ed McCully, and Pete Fleming—evangelical missionaries who were attempting to make contact and share the good news of Jesus with a fierce unreached indigenous tribe of people called the Waorani. The team had previously made contact from the air with members of the Waorani, and so the Waorani were prepared for their return. Around 3:00 p.m. on the day the five men landed, several members of the tribe burst from the trees brandishing spears. Within moments, each of the five Americans had been murdered at the end of a spear. Their bodies were left in the sun.

Although the missionaries had guns with them, they allowed themselves to be killed.[1]

It's obvious to everyone that humanity has a problem. Christians say the problem is sin. For secular folks the problem is systemic injustice or a lack of education or an unequal distribution of resources. But it's still obvious to everyone that humanity has a problem. The burning question is, What is to be done?

Our pop-culture answers to that question often boil down to some version of the hippie response: "Peace and love, man."

That sounds good, but while saying "all we need is love" sounds nice in a three-minute and forty-five-second radio hit, it isn't a very useful sentiment in the real world. Life in the real world is nasty, brutish, and short. In the real world, nice guys finish last, the good die young, and might makes right. It's easy to talk about peace and love in a pop song, but in the real world it seems as if in the end love just gets you killed. The story of the deaths of those five American missionaries at the end of the spear in the Amazon jungle could be seen as a sobering example of how life actually works. If you reach out with arms open, you're merely opening yourself up to be speared.

Throughout this book, we have been using the phrase *go first* in a particular sense: To go first means to move in love toward another, palms up, arms open, defenseless. To go first means choosing to act and not waiting to react. Naturally, we are all inclined to protect ourselves, to wait and watch—"Is this person friend or foe?" If the other person persuades us that he is friendly, then we will respond with friendliness. If the other person is a foe, then it's fight or flight. But going first upends our normal inclination to associate with those we know and avoid those we don't. When you make the first move, you overturn the status quo and open up new possibilities. It's the only way things ever really change—through sacrificial love. But because going first requires sacrifice, it isn't easy and comes at a great cost.

Going first can cost you everything. It's the early Christian who gets the lion. We cannot talk about loving the way Jesus loved without accepting the possibility of martyrdom, literally and figuratively. Though it may not be a reality any of us face in our lifetimes, we still must be prepared to die. When we go first toward the other, the very act of moving toward them makes us vulnerable. That vulnerability may break through the other's hard heart, the way Judah's sacrifice pierced Joseph's heart. But going first may also set you up to be killed.

On the morning of March 24, 2018, an Islamic terrorist killed two people and then took a cashier hostage at a supermarket in the small southern French town of Trèbes. One of the first police officers to respond to the calls of distress was Lieutenant Colonel Arnaud Beltrame, a member of the French national police force. Lt. Col. Beltrame persuaded the terrorist to agree to let the woman go if he exchanged places with her. Laying down his weapons but keeping his phone on so other police officers could hear what was happening, Beltrame walked into the supermarket as the screaming hostage fled. Two hours later, at the sound of gunfire, the officers surrounding the supermarket stormed in and killed the gunman. They found Beltrame seriously wounded, and he died later that day. He had been shot, but it was the knife wound to his throat that killed him.

"Of whom the world was not worthy" (Heb. 11:38 ESV).

LOVE ALWAYS COMES WITH A COST

We started this book with a question, What do we do now? In a divided and polarized world, how do we reach the people on the other side, the people who don't like us, the people who hate us? As the church, how do we fulfill our mission to reach the world for Jesus? How do we win over our post-Christian culture? How do we evangelize in the negative world? The answer: If we want to change the world, we have to go first, because love goes first. We have looked carefully at the different options the church has, drawing from Scripture to discern the dead ends, and have come to the clear conclusion that the only way forward for the church is to go. We have discussed why going first has such power to upend the status quo and open up new possibilities. We have seen example after example of people choosing to go first, and what happened as a result.

But before we conclude, we need to understand the very real risks and costs that come from going first. There is a reason the natural human tendency is to hang back, to wait and see. There is a reason a boxer always keeps his gloves up—he needs to protect his face. If he drops his guard and drops his gloves, he is liable to be knocked down. When you move toward another person in love—when you move first to send the text, or make the phone call, or walk across the room to say hello, or bake the cake, or turn toward your estranged spouse, or forgive, or try to tell people about the life-giving death of Jesus in a world of violence and fear—you make yourself tremendously vulnerable. Love always comes with a cost. None of this should surprise us, however, because Jesus already told us all of this: "Then Jesus said to his disciples, 'Whoever wants to be my disciple must deny themselves and take up their cross and follow me. For whoever wants to save their life will lose it, but whoever loses their life for me will find it. What good will it be for someone to gain the whole world, yet forfeit their soul? Or what can anyone give in exchange for their soul?'" (Matt. 16:24–26).

We cannot say that Jesus did not warn us: What it takes to follow him will at times feel like a crucifixion. Taking up one's cross is the faithful act of obediently doing the very thing that feels like death. Will discipleship always require martyrdom? No. But it will always come with a cost. And let us be clear: This will hurt. This is because every act of sacrificial love involves a degree of dying to self no matter what.

If you decide to go first, you will get hurt. It will sting. You'll be misunderstood. People will try to use you. Going first will hurt your pride and waste your time. You will be rejected and blamed. If you pursue reconciliation, be prepared for it to be a painful failure. To smile at your spouse for the first time in a year will not be easy. When you decide to forgo your right to get even and to forgive the person who wronged you, it will taste like fire. Love is all well and good in the abstract, but in actuality it burns. Perhaps this is why so many people seem to prefer the world's sentimental definition of love, because sentiment doesn't really cost that much. But if you choose to love in the way of Jesus, you will pay a heavy price. Jesus, after all, was crucified.

NOT A VICTIM BUT A SACRIFICE

Jesus, however, was not a victim. He willingly gave his life to reconcile the world to God. It was a choice: "The reason my

Father loves me is that I lay down my life—only to take it up again. No one takes it from me, but I lay it down of my own accord. I have authority to lay it down and authority to take it up again. This command I received from my Father" (John 10:17–18). Jesus is very clear: He freely chose to die to free the world from the power of sin and death and thereby bring the world back to God.

We now live in a time when victimhood is valorized. This is because our culture has adopted Christian values but rejected Christ, so we have taken the gospel's idea of noble sacrifice and turned it into victim worship. In modern America, if you want to gain cultural power, you claim to be a victim. The more adept you are at playing the victim, the more power you will gain. Christians are sadly not exempt from this temptation. This is a problem, because if we in the church adopt the mantle of victim, we will find ourselves stuck, unable to go forward.

There is this great scene in Exodus after the Hebrews have left Egypt, following the terrible tenth plague and the deaths of the firstborn in Egypt, but before they have crossed the Red Sea. Pharaoh has sent chariots after the Israelites, and it looks as if there will be a slaughter. The Israelites cry out in fear to the Lord. But look at what the Lord says to them: "The LORD said to Moses, 'Why do you cry to me? Tell the people of Israel to go forward'" (Ex. 14:15 ESV).

The problem with a victim mindset is that it keeps you from moving forward. The problem with victimhood is that it keeps a person down. This is why going first is such a powerful posture. When you move first in love, you are not reacting as a victim, you are acting as an agent created in God's image. And there is tremendous power and dignity in such action.

But though Jesus was not a victim, he was a sacrifice. Out of obedience to the Father and in order to love the world, he gave himself up to be crucified. Crucifixion is what love ultimately requires. If we will follow Jesus, then we will have to follow him to the cross.

THE BLOOD OF THE MARTYRS IS
THE SEED OF THE CHURCH

And yet there is no other way. If you and I want to change the world, we simply have to go first, come what may. The church father Tertullian famously said that "the blood of the martyrs is the seed of the church." What he meant was that even nasty persecution has a way of causing the gospel message to spread. But I think you can take his point and expand it: The only way forward is the way of the cross. Sacrifice is necessary for the gospel to spread; if we want to love people, that love comes with a cost. If we want to love people, we have to be willing to die for them. And not just for our friends but for our enemies. Sometimes that means a death of pride or status or security. Sometimes—Christ have mercy—it may mean actual death, like that of Nate Saint in the Amazon jungle with his unused firearm, or Lt. Col. Arnaud Beltrame in a French supermarket, cell phone in his pocket.

Jesus had many beautiful things to say about love, and

he told remarkable parables such as the one about the Good Samaritan and the one about the Prodigal Son. And yet all of that nice language seemed irrelevant at best and delusional at worst when he was crucified. It is all well and good to talk about the brotherhood of man and loving one's enemies when you aren't getting killed, but when you end up on a Roman cross, somehow all of those nice words seem a lot less compelling. "If you want peace, prepare for war" is the old Latin saying, and it strikes me that there is a lot of wisdom in that sentiment—the world is a violent, nasty place, and therefore it is in your interest to be nastier and more violent than your neighbors. And to let them know it.

On Good Friday, it certainly seemed as if Jesus' beautiful words were buried with his body.

THE END OF THE SPEAR

In a remarkable series of events, within a year after the deaths of the five missionaries on the riverbank in the Amazonian jungle, other missionaries did reach the Waorani people with the gospel, and several members of the tribe eventually became Christians. Marj Saint, Nate's widow, stayed in Ecuador with her fatherless children, including her son, Steve, who spent time in the summers around the very people responsible for his father's death. In an absolutely astounding twist that only the Holy Spirit could make possible, Steve ended up being baptized in the same river in which his father had been murdered, by the same men who had murdered his father, who had now become followers of Jesus. The fierce warriors of the Waorani had become followers of Jesus, and their way of life changed from one of war to one of peace. It was the end of the spear.

Arnaud Beltrame's death caused a sensation in France. French president Emmanuel Macron posthumously awarded Beltrame the highest award of the French Republic. He was given a state funeral. The story of his sacrifice captivated the interest of people all over Europe, and in fact all over the world. Why would a stranger offer his life for someone he had never met?

Like much of the rest of Europe, mainstream French culture today is overwhelmingly secular. The beautiful and breathtaking churches and cathedrals that are found all across the country are largely empty on Sunday mornings, and many people are raised in nonreligious homes. Beltrame's early life was not that different from those of so many of his country-men. But, in his thirties, Beltrame had been received into the Roman Catholic Church, and it seemed that, in the years since his first Communion at age thirty-three until his death at age forty-four, he had become increasingly devout. He had taken a religious pilgrimage and was planning a church wedding that would have taken place the summer after his death.

When Nate Saint and the other men died, it may have looked as if all of our fears about going first were finally realized. "When you go first," we might think, "that's what happens—you die at the end of a spear." When Arnaud Beltrame walked into the supermarket, it might have looked like a useless sacrifice.

But the Holy Spirit is at work, and he is working all things for good for those who love God. God's love has been poured out on the world, and that love is unstoppable. On Good Friday, it looked as if Jesus' teachings were a comforting dream.

After Easter Sunday, though, we see that Jesus was right about *everything*.

To the early church, Jesus' resurrection vindicated everything he did and taught. Very few modern Christians think of the resurrection as vindication, but that is certainly what the early church understood it to be. If God raised Jesus from the dead by the power of the Holy Spirit, then it means that God was showing the world that Jesus was right and the powers of sin and death were wrong.

If Jesus had stayed in the tomb, there would be no reason to believe that love wins or that we should go first. But since the tomb is empty, it proves that love is stronger than evil and that actions done in love will be vindicated by God. The reason we go first is because God so loved the world that he sent his only son and then raised him from the dead. Be confident, therefore, brothers and sisters, that any actions done in love will be vindicated, regardless of how things look from your present viewpoint. We can see now that Nate Saint's martyrdom had a purpose in the fulfillment of the Great Commission, and it may be that the story of the sacrifice of Arnaud Beltrame will be part of what God uses to pierce through the hard heart of secular Europe. If you want to change the world, you have to go first, because love goes first.

And love never fails.

IN THE END, YOU JUST HAVE TO GO (WHAT OTHER OPTION DO WE REALLY HAVE?)

The world resists easy categorization, and the naïve and the simple and the unprepared will be ground up and spit out by it. I believe that today the church is facing an unprecedented challenge and will continue to face it for decades to come—the challenge of evangelizing a post-Christian culture. What we have done in the past is not going to work in the future. We must have a new strategy for evangelization. Or, to be precise, we must learn to embrace the oldest one of all.

Yes, this strategy contains risks. When we go first, we make ourselves vulnerable. Jesus went first to the world, and the world crucified him. The early church went first to reach Jew and gentile, and many followers of Jesus were martyred for their attempts. The willingness to sacrifice oneself for the sake of others was the way of the church in the first century, and, if we are going to reach the world, it will have to be the way of the church in the twenty-first century, too.

Robert Graves was an English officer on the Western Front in World War I, and he recalls in his memoir *Goodbye to All That* how he concluded that the safest course of action was one that at first would seem to be the most dangerous: volunteering for night patrols in no-man's-land.

> After this I went on patrol fairly often, finding that the only thing respected in young officers was personal courage. Besides, I had cannily worked it out like this. My best way

of lasting through to the end of the war would be to get wounded. The best time to get wounded would be at night and in the open, with rifle fire more or less unaimed and my whole body exposed. Best, also, to get wounded when there was no rush on the dressing-station services, and while the back areas were not being heavily shelled. Best to get wounded, therefore, on a night patrol in a quiet sector. One could usually manage to crawl into a shell hole until help arrived.[2]

I love his matter-of-fact conclusion that if you are going to get wounded anyway, you might as well move forward in action.

That's what life is like for all of us—no one makes it out of here alive. There are ultimately no safe spaces, and everyone will be knocked down by the world and will bear the wounds to show for it. Life is difficult for all of us. Yes, to go first for others is costly. But what other choice do we really have? In light of the resurrection of Jesus and the promises of God, why not resolve to go first, come what may? Considering the tremendous message with which we are entrusted—the love of God for the world—and the desperate situation in which the world finds itself, is there really any other choice but to do whatever it takes to get the world to hear the good news about Jesus? Why not decide to live a life of action, rather than simply reaction? Why not use your one life in such a way that your choice to go first will open up new possibilities for the grace of God? Why not be on the front foot? After all, what else is there? Why not go first?

DISCUSSION QUESTIONS

1. What is the difference between a victim and a sacrifice?

2. Why did Jesus emphasize the fact that he freely gave up his life, that it was not taken from him?

3. "Love always comes with a cost." Do you agree with that statement? Why or why not?

4. Why did Jesus warn his disciples that crucifixion was the cost of discipleship? What does Jesus mean when he says that you must take up your cross?

5. What did Tertullian mean by his famous phrase "The blood of the martyrs is the seed of the church?"

6. Is there anyone in your life who sacrificed so that you would know the love of God?

7. What is the importance of the resurrection in the story of Jesus? What would have been the message had the Gospels ended at the crucifixion?

EPILOGUE

Post-Christian or Pre-Awakening?

Sometime around AD 400 a young British Christian man living on the west coast of Britain was kidnapped by Irish raiders and sold into slavery in Ireland. Ireland had not yet been evangelized, and the young man lived as a slave among fierce pagan peoples for six miserable years until he escaped and made his way back across the Irish Sea and was reunited with his family. His autobiography has miraculously survived through the ages, and here he is describing his return home: "A few years later I was again with my parents in Britain. They welcomed me as a son, and they pleaded with me that, after all the many tribulations I had undergone, I should never leave them again."

Shortly after his homecoming, the man had a vision in the night in which a letter was delivered to him. As he read the letter in the vision, he realized the letter was the voice of the Irish people: "They called out as it were with one voice: 'We beg you, holy boy, to come and walk again among us.' This touched my heart deeply, and I could not read any further; I woke up then."[1]

After hearing their desperate plea and despite his family's tears, the young man resolved to return to Ireland as a missionary of Christ.

The framework we have been using is that we are entering a post-Christian world. American culture has changed over the past several decades from having a positive view of Christianity to having a negative view of Christianity, and if the church is going to be faithful to its mission, our strategies for reaching people for Jesus will have to change, too. The argument I have been making in this book is that the way forward is to move forward, to go first. If you want to change the world, you have to go first, because love goes first. In a post-Christian world, this is the only path before us.

But what if the framework we have been working with is wrong? What if the world is less post-Christian than it is pre-awakening?

SAINT PATRICK, APOSTLE TO THE IRISH

That young British Christian man was named Patrick, and today he is known as the patron saint of Ireland. Though Patrick was not the first man ever to take the gospel to the Irish, he was the man most responsible for the evangelization of Ireland. Can you imagine the moral authority Patrick had as he interacted with the Irish? He had been a slave in their land, escaped, and then freely returned to tell them about Jesus. Patrick moved toward the Irish, and the future of the world was changed.

Every breath we take is proof: God isn't done yet. And again, today, just as in prior times, I believe the Lord is looking for people who are willing to go toward others in the name of Jesus. This is God's plan to reach the world.

It worked before, and it will work again.

And Jesus went throughout all the cities and villages, teaching in their synagogues and proclaiming the gospel of the kingdom and healing every disease and every affliction. When he saw the crowds, he had compassion for them, because they were harassed and helpless, like sheep without a shepherd. Then he said to his disciples, "The harvest is plentiful, but the laborers are few; therefore pray earnestly to the Lord of the harvest to send out laborers into his harvest."

—MATTHEW 9:35–38 ESV

Let's go.

NOTES

Introduction

1. Mike Tyson (@MikeTyson), "Everyone has a plan till they get punched in the mouth," X, October 17, 2018, https://x.com /MikeTyson/status/1052665864401633299.

Chapter 1: Welcome to the Negative World

1. To see the ad, search YouTube for "He Gets Us—Love Your Enemies." It's fifty-nine seconds long and well worth watching.

2. AJ Willingham, "The Truth Behind the 'He Gets Us' Ads for Jesus Airing During the Super Bowl," CNN, last updated February 13, 2023, www.cnn.com/2023/02/11/us/he-gets-us -super-bowl-commercials-cec/index.html.

3. *Discipleship* is the term for the second part of the command: "Teach them to obey everything I taught you." Or to put it another way, evangelism is creating disciples of Jesus, and discipleship is training disciples to live like Jesus.

4. Jim Collins and Jerry I. Porras, *Built to Last: Successful Habits of Visionary Companies* (New York: Harper Business, 1994), 93.

5. Aaron M. Renn, *Life in the Negative World: Confronting Challenges in an Anti-Christian Culture* (Grand Rapids: Zondervan Reflective, 2024).

6. Carol Tucker, "The 1950s—Powerful Years for Religion," *USC Today*, June 16, 1997, https://today.usc.edu/the-1950s-powerful -years-for-religion.

7. Laura Hillenbrand, *Unbroken: A World War II Story of Survival, Resilience, and Redemption* (New York: Random House, 2010), 372–73.

8. Linton Weeks, "What Obama's Choice of Rick Warren Really

Means," NPR, December 18, 2008, www.npr.org/2008/12/18
/98453190/what-obamas-choice-of-rick-warren-really-means.

9. Sheryl Gay Stolberg, "Minister Backs out of Speech at
Inaugural," *New York Times*, January 10, 2013, www.nytimes
.com/2013/01/11/us/politics/minister-withdraws-from
-inaugural-program-after-controversy-over-comments-on
-gay-rights.html.

10. Michael Martinez, "The Evolution of the Nation's 'First Gay
President,'" CNN, last updated March 4, 2013, www.cnn.com
/2013/03/02/politics/obama-evolution-gay-marriage/index.html.

11. Zeke J. Miller, "Axelrod: Obama Misled Nation When He
Opposed Gay Marriage in 2008," *Time*, February 10, 2015,
https://time.com/3702584/gay-marriage-axelrod-obama.

Chapter 2: Three Dead Ends, One Way Forward

1. Steven H. Werlin, "Masada," in *Lexham Bible Dictionary*
(Bellingham, WA: Lexham Press, 2016).

2. Tom Holland, *Dominion: How the Christian Revolution
Remade the World* (New York: Hachette, 2019).

3. Craig Keener, *Revelation*, NIV Application Commentary
(Grand Rapids: Zondervan, 2000), 158–59.

4. Acts 2:37.

5. The Greek word for *witness* is the word from which we get our
English word *martyr*.

Chapter 3: Why Feelings Don't Care About Your Facts

1. Jonathan Haidt, *The Happiness Hypothesis: Finding Modern
Truth in Ancient Wisdom* (New York: Basic, 2006).

2. Ben Shapiro, *Facts Don't Care About Your Feelings* (Hermosa
Beach, CA: Creators, 2019).

3. Dividing up history into eras is an arbitrary exercise, because
everything is caused by something else that came before it.
Nevertheless, using shorthand phrases such as "the Scientific
Revolution" does make talking about the past a bit easier.

4. Carl Trueman's 2022 book *Strange New World* would be a good place to start to learn in more detail how these philosophical changes came to be.
5. Mark 15:7.
6. John 8:31–32.
7. Luke 18:11.
8. "America's Divided Mind: Understanding the Psychology That Drives Us Apart," Beyond Conflict, June 2020, https://beyondconflictint.org/americas-divided-mind.

Chapter 4: Other People Are More Scared of You Than You Are of Them

1. Robert Coram, *Boyd: The Fighter Pilot Who Changed the Art of War* (New York: Back Bay Books, 2002), 7.
2. Wikipedia, "OODA Loop," last updated August 30, 2024, https://en.wikipedia.org/wiki/OODA_loop.
3. Ian Cross, "Ian Cross Introduces New Research on Music, Speech and Interaction," *Music @ Cambridge: Research*, April 21, 2021, https://musicatcambridge.wordpress.com/2021/04/21/ian-cross-introduces-the-latest-research-on-music-speech-and-interaction/?utm_source=ayjay&utm_medium=email.
4. Mark 12:13–17.
5. Luke 10:25–37.
6. He'll say something similar in John 7:37–39: "On the last and greatest day of the festival, Jesus stood and said in a loud voice, 'Let anyone who is thirsty come to me and drink. Whoever believes in me, as Scripture has said, rivers of living water will flow from within them.' By this he meant the Spirit, whom those who believed in him were later to receive. Up to that time the Spirit had not been given, since Jesus had not yet been glorified."
7. See John 1:14.

Chapter 5: Love

1. Of the Ten Commandments, only two are positive commands: "Remember the Sabbath" and "Honor your father and mother." The other eight commands are prohibitions: "Do not steal," "Do not murder," and so on.
2. "The Law" is a shorthand phrase that the biblical authors use to refer to the Torah, the first five books of the Old Testament, which contains instructions that God gave to Moses in the wilderness so that the Israelites would know how to live as God's people. In Hebrew, *torah* means "teaching" or "instruction."
3. Matthew 22:34–40.
4. I think it would be fair to say that the Bible sees the erotic as being a particular type or subset of love, and not love in general.
5. Some portions of the books of Daniel and Ezra were written in Aramaic.
6. Michael Reeves, *Delighting in the Trinity: An Introduction to the Christian Faith* (Downers Grove, IL: InterVarsity, 2012), 45.
7. Reeves, *Trinity*, 28.
8. Thomas Aquinas, *Summa Theologica I.20.1*, Project Gutenberg, last updated January 3, 2021, www.gutenberg.org/cache/epub/17611/pg17611-images.html.
9. Andy Crouch, "Overcoming Our Greatest Affliction," posted September 2, 2018, by THINQ Media, YouTube, www.youtube.com/watch?v=KHGwOYzUw9o.

Chapter 6: Going First in the Word and in the World

1. Hope Schreiber, "'Lead with Kindness.' Woman Writes Letter to Noisy Neighbor and Bakes Him a Cake, Leading to New Friendship," Yahoo Life, December 23, 2018, www.yahoo.com/lifestyle/lead-kindness-woman-writes-letter-bakes-noisy-neighbor-cake-leading-new-friendship-210005329.html.
2. Presumably, the youngest son, Benjamin, is still a child at this time and is not present when this incident occurs.
3. Jonah 4:1–3.

4. The end of the book of Jonah is often forgotten: Instead of being joyful, Jonah is bitterly angry and complains to the Lord that this is the outcome he feared: "But to Jonah this seemed very wrong, and he became angry. He prayed to the Lord, 'Isn't this what I said, Lord, when I was still at home? That is what I tried to forestall by fleeing to Tarshish. I knew that you are a gracious and compassionate God, slow to anger and abounding in love, a God who relents from sending calamity. Now, Lord, take away my life, for it is better for me to die than to live'" (Jonah 4:1–3). Jonah would rather die than see his enemies repent! There is a lesson there for all of us.

5. Jesus, the master storyteller, does not actually tell us how the story ends but leaves us with the drama unresolved.

6. Search "Bong Joon Ho Accepts the Oscar for Directing"—you won't regret it.

7. Todd Archer, "Why Jerry Jones Put Jimmy Johnson in Cowboys Ring of Honor," ESPN, December 27, 2023, www .espn.com/nfl/story/_/id/39186699/why-jerry-jones-put-jimmy -johnson-dallas-cowboys-ring-honor.

8. "Jerry Jones Tells Jimmy Johnson He Will be Inducted into the Cowboys' Ring of Honor," posted November 19, 2023, by NFL on Fox, YouTube, www.youtube.com/watch?v=_YKltkF6Mzk.

9. "Jimmy Johnson Ring of Honor Induction," posted December 30, 2023, by Dallas Cowboys, YouTube, www.youtube .com/watch?v=xObYEwWoXS8.

10. David McCullough, *John Adams* (New York: Simon and Schuster, 2001), 646.

11. McCullough, *John Adams*, 602–3.

12. Elizabeth Wiley, "'I Forgive You': Botham Jean's Brother, Amber Guyger Embrace Following Witness Impact Statement," WFAA, last updated October 3, 2019, www.wfaa.com/article /news/special-reports/botham-jean/botham-jeans-brother -amber-guyger-embrace-following-witness-impact -statement/287-c70ff4b7-aafd-448a-b24a-f67b173af40d.

Chapter 7: The Only Thing It Takes to Go First Is Everything

1. Kathryn T. Long, *God in the Rainforest: A Tale of Martyrdom and Redemption in Amazonian Ecuador* (New York: Oxford University Press, 2019), 21.
2. Robert Graves, *Goodbye to All That*, Everyman's Library (New York: Knopf, 2018), 134.

Epilogue

1. "Saint Patrick's *Confessio*," Saint Patrick's *Confessio* Hypertext Stack Project, Royal Irish Academy, accessed March 24, 2025, www.confessio.ie/etexts/confessio_english.